Thomas Carlyle, Jane Welsh Carlyle

Early Letters of Jane Welsh Carlyle

Together With a Few of Later Years and Some of Thomas Carlyle

Thomas Carlyle, Jane Welsh Carlyle

Early Letters of Jane Welsh Carlyle
Together With a Few of Later Years and Some of Thomas Carlyle

ISBN/EAN: 9783337019181

Printed in Europe, USA, Canada, Australia, Japan

Cover: Foto ©ninafisch / pixelio.de

More available books at **www.hansebooks.com**

EARLY LETTERS

OF

JANE WELSH CARLYLE

FACSIMILE OF SILHOUETTE PORTRAIT OF JANE WELSH

FORMERLY IN THE POSSESSION OF ELIZA STODART.

Frontispiece.

EARLY LETTERS

OF

JANE WELSH CARLYLE

TOGETHER WITH A FEW OF LATER YEARS

AND SOME OF

THOMAS CARLYLE

All Hitherto Unpublished

EDITED BY

DAVID G. RITCHIE, M.A.

Fellow and Tutor of Jesus College, Oxford

London
SWAN SONNENSCHEIN & CO.
PATERNOSTER SQUARE
1889

BUTLER & TANNER,
THE SELWOOD PRINTING WORKS,
FROME, AND LONDON.

PREFACE.

It was in the beginning of last October that I first saw any of the following letters. Most of them are addressed to Eliza Stodart, my great-aunt. I knew of the existence of letters from Mrs. Carlyle to her, but until they came into the hands of my mother and myself I could not know that it would seem a duty to English literature to make them public. The desire to do so might have been overbalanced by other considerations, had not the private life of Mr. and Mrs. Carlyle been already so much exposed to the general gaze; but since the case has, so to speak, come before the court (whether rightly or wrongly I need not discuss), it is only fair that important evidence should not be withheld. It will be noticed that nearly four-fifths of these letters belong to the years before 1834, the date at which the letters published by Mr. Froude in *Letters and Memorials of Jane Welsh Carlyle* begin: so that here, for the first time, may be read an account, brief and yet abounding in detail, of the earlier years of Jane Welsh, from her father's death till her marriage, and of the life at Craigenputtoch, as seen from her own point of view and described in her own words. I have, indeed, the less hesitation in publishing these letters, because of the pleasing light in which, on the whole, they show both Carlyle and his wife; and, in saying this, I would call attention to the fact, that all the letters to Eliza Stodart are printed *without omissions*. Any omission, even of what might be thought

trivialities, would have little justification on purely
literary grounds, and would certainly have diminished
the value of the letters as materials for the proper
estimation of the intellect and character of this singularly brilliant woman. It has indeed been thought
unnecessary to give in full some names of persons, who
have not already been brought before the world in
Carlyle's *Reminiscences* and in the other Carlyle literature, at least where such names could be suppressed or
concealed without loss and without risk of ambiguity.
Again, it would only have irritated the reader to repro-
duce all the oddities of Jane Welsh's spelling and
punctuation.[1] The spelling has been retained where
there could be the slightest uncertainty as to the persons and places meant. Her frequent underlinings
have been carefully followed; and in many instances
her rather wavering use of capitals (which she sometimes, apparently, employs for emphasis)—though in
this matter it is difficult to find any perfectly satisfactory principle. In the case of the twelve letters of
Carlyle, which came into my hands along with those
of his wife, every detail has been reproduced as
exactly as possible.

Very few of Jane Welsh's letters are dated, and most

---

[1] "Persue," "dimest," "seperation," "comit," "colera,"
"gohst," "staid" (for "stayed"), "died" (for "dyed"),
"earings," "abomminations," may serve as specimens, and as
consolation for those whose souls are vexed by English ortho-
graphy. The spelling of proper names is frequently even more
eccentric; *e.g.* "Carslile," "Pailey," "Lacedomnians," "Walen-
stein." I call attention to such matters, because they prove the
rapidity and carelessness with which the most brilliant letters
were dashed off.

of the earlier ones are without postmarks. Hence the arrangement has been, to a great extent, matter of conjecture, and not always very easy. I am fairly satisfied with the results reached. The only cases in which I still feel any uncertainty are those of Letters III., V., IX., XXIX., LII. But this element of uncertainty is so slight, that the letters as arranged may be safely taken to represent the mental history of the writer. As merely the editor, I think that my duty ends with putting the material in a convenient shape before the reader, and that it is better that I should say nothing here in the somewhat painful controversy that has raged round the characters of Carlyle and his wife.

What was the cousinship between Jane Welsh and her correspondent Eliza Stodart I do not know, nor in what way their youthful friendship began. Eliza Stodart lived mostly at 22 George Square, Edinburgh, with her maternal uncle, Mr. John Bradfute,[2] known to his young relatives as "Bradie." Mr. Bradfute belonged to the firm of Bell & Bradfute, booksellers,

---

[2] "Mrs. Bradfute," in a passage quoted from Carlyle by Mr. Froude (*Thomas Carlyle*, A. i., p. 129) must be a misreading. Mr. Bradfute was unmarried, and Eliza Stodart kept house for him. In a letter of 1833, during the Edinburgh visit, Carlyle writes to his brother John, "I am to go and dine with old uncle Bradfute (at a *precise* moment)": on which passage Prof. Norton's note (*Letters* [Second Series], ii., p. 72) is as follows: "A relation of Mrs. Carlyle, a partner in the firm of Bell & Bradfute," etc. There *may* have been a relationship with Jane Welsh; but I do not think Carlyle's words necessarily imply that. In writing to Eliza Stodart, Jane Welsh always calls him "*Your* Uncle."

Bank Street, Edinburgh. The business of the firm was, in Mr. Bradfute's old age, mostly carried on by Mr. Sam Aitken, frequently mentioned in these letters. He was a cousin (more or less) of the Rev. David Aitken, who married Eliza Stodart in 1836. So far as I know, he was not related to the Dumfriesshire Aitkens, with whom the Carlyles were and are connected. My grandmother, the "Maggie" (and afterwards the "Mrs. John," *i.e.* Mrs. John Dudgeon) of these letters, who was a sister of Eliza Stodart, but considerably younger, told my mother that Jane Welsh "used to go to 22 George Square on Saturdays from school, and took her gloves and stockings to be mended." But the school time in Edinburgh is a doubtful feature in this tradition, though the "gloves and stockings" suggest some residence of a *not* home-like kind. There is no allusion to any Edinburgh school in these letters, nor in anything already published about Jane Welsh. And the opinion among some Haddington correspondents, who have kindly answered questions of mine, is that she never was at any school except at Haddington. She was taught at the Grammar School, partly along with the boys, by Edward Irving and his successor, the Rev. James Brown. Carlyle in his *Reminiscences* tells of her being for a short time at a boarding school, but in Haddington itself. "Once," he says, "I cannot say in what year, nor for how many months,—but perhaps about six or eight, her age perhaps eight or nine,—her mother thinking it good, she was sent away to another House of the Town, to *board* with some kind of Ex-Governess Person, who had married some Ex-Military ditto, and professed to be able to educate young ladies and form their *manners* ('better' thought the mother, 'than with nothing but *men* as here at home!')—and in this place, with a Miss Something, a friend and playmate of like age, she was fixed down, for a good few months, and suffered, she and the companion manifold disgust, even hardships, even want of proper food; wholly without complaining (too proud and loyal for that); till it was by some accident found out, and instantly put an end to."[3] I have no reason to think that Eliza Stodart was the companion in this unhappy experience. If Carlyle is right in placing this "House" in Haddington, this teacher of "young ladies" cannot be the Mrs. Seton referred to in Letter III., p. 9. Perhaps Jane Welsh may have spent some time in Edinburgh, partly amusing herself,[4] but partly acquiring "accomplishments," such as music and drawing, which would fall outside the usual course of the Haddington Grammar School.

But this is mere conjecture. From these letters themselves it can only be inferred that there was some claim of kinship and the custom of mutual visits as the basis of an intimate friendship, which lasted through many years, though in later life it suffered diminution, as, alas! too easily happens, through long separation, long silence, and divergence of interests. The few references to "Bess Stodart" in *Letters and Memorials*[5] display (to say the least) no strong feeling of affection; but the letter written by Mrs. Carlyle

---

[3] *Reminiscences*, ed. Norton, i., p. 74. The passage is omitted in Mr. Froude's edition.

[4] "I liked Edinburgh last time as well as I did at sixteen (you know how well that was)."—Letter XXIV., p. 149.

[5] i., p. 103; ii., pp. 47, 357; iii., p. 313.

(numbered LV. in this book) in the month before her
death proves that the old days were not forgotten.

There *may* have been some other letters to Eliza
Stodart besides those preserved (see note at beginning
to Letter XLVI.); but I think it is clear from the
letters themselves that hardly anything can have been
destroyed.

The letters here numbered LI. and LII. I am
allowed to use by the kindness of Mr. R. Scot Skirving,
of Edinburgh, about whom and to whom they were
written. Letter LI. has only been preserved in a copy,
the original apparently being lost. Of all the other
letters I have had the originals before me. For Letter
LIV., which contains an interesting reminiscence of
childhood, I have to thank Mrs. Pott, of Knowe-
south in Teviotdale, to whom it was addressed. She
is a cousin of Mrs. Carlyle, and was then Mrs. Pringle,
and living in Dumfriesshire. The earlier part of this
letter,—condolences on the death of a relative,—I have
omitted, solely because it would have required explana-
tions about persons not otherwise mentioned in this
volume. This is the only case in which I have left
out any part of a letter.

The silhouette which is reproduced as the frontispiece
belongs to a set of three in my mother's possession,
about which there is an unwavering tradition that one
of them is a portrait of Jane Welsh. They were sub-
mitted to the judgment of several experts, who decided
without hesitation in favour of this one, by comparing
them with a profile photograph of Mrs. Carlyle, and
with the engraving of the early portrait which forms
the frontispiece of the second volume of Mr. Froude's

Life of Carlyle and of the second volume of Professor Norton's *Early Letters of Thomas Carlyle.*

The notes have been intended, in the first place, to enable those who are familiar with the already considerable mass of Carlyle correspondence and biography to fit this new material into its proper position, and, in the second place, to throw light upon the numerous literary and other allusions in the letters. In referring to Mr. Froude's *Life of Carlyle*, I have, for the sake of brevity, described the *History of the First Forty Years* as A., and the *History of his Life in London* as B. In referring to the *Reminiscences*, I have given the pages in the editions both of Mr. Froude and of Professor Norton; where this is not done, it is because the passage is not to be found in Mr. Froude's edition. I have called the two volumes of Carlyle's *Letters*, lately published by Professor Norton, "Second Series," to distinguish them from the *Early Letters*. Some matters I have been unable to explain. Many, who could easily have solved my difficulties, have in recent years passed into silence. Doubtless, by using much more time, and by troubling many more persons, I could have made the commentary more complete; but there are, perhaps, some readers who will even be grateful to me that the notes are not more numerous: and I, in turn, shall be grateful to any one who will point out errors or clear up obscurities.

I have to thank many kind correspondents in Scotland, who answered queries contained in two letters which I sent to the Editor of the *Scotsman*.[6] I am also

---

[6] *Note* 2 on Letter XI. (p. 80) and *Note* 3 on Letter XLIV. (p. 264) are *entirely* due to answers received to these letters.

indebted to some of my friends for help and suggestion on special points; amongst others, to Professor W. P. Ker and Mr. C. H. Firth. I have had the great advantage of consulting Dr. J. A. H. Murray with regard to many of the interesting Scotticisms which Mrs. Carlyle uses. Some of my obligations to others who have given me valuable assistance are acknowledged in the notes concerned. Above all, I owe a debt of gratitude and thanks to Dr. G. Birkbeck Hill, who has read through all my proofs, supplied me with a clue to many of the literary allusions, and generously given me throughout the benefit of his experience as an editor and of his knowledge of English literature.

I have also to thank Mr. Froude for kindly consenting, as the executor of Mr. and Mrs. Carlyle, to the publication of these letters; and my sister-in-law, Miss Macdonell, for carefully transcribing them for the printer under my direction.

DAVID G. RITCHIE.

OXFORD,
   May 19*th*, 1889.

TABLE OF CONTENTS.

LETTER		PAGE
I.	[Autumn, 1819.] From Haddington. *Jane Welsh to Eliza Stodart.* Her father's recent death.—At church with her mother	1
II.	[Autumn, 1819.] From Haddington. *Jane Welsh to Eliza Stodart.* The loss of her father.—His grave in the ruins	4
III.	[Early in 1820?] From Haddington. *Jane Welsh to Eliza Stodart.* Teaching her aunt and two other pupils.—The memory of her father.—Visitors, Benjamin B—— and others	7
IV.	Oct. 14, 1820. From Liverpool. *Jane Welsh to Eliza Stodart.* The journey to Liverpool.—Her uncle Robert.—The uncle and aunt at Liverpool.—Remarks on Liverpool and Carlisle	14
V.	March 8 [1821?]. From Haddington. *Jane Welsh to Eliza Stodart.* Haddington is very dull, but full of childhood's memories.—A quondam lover's visit.—Dr. Fyffe.—A hubbub in church.—On letter-writing.—A *P.S.* on marmalade and other matters	19
VI.	[1821 or 1822.] From Haddington. *Jane Welsh to Eliza Stodart.* Impressions of *La Nouvelle Héloïse.*—Wanted a "Wolmar" or a "St. Preux."—"I will write a novel."—Mr. Buchanan.—Thomas Carlyle considered as a St. Preux.—George Rennie	29
VII.	[Early in 1822.] From Haddington. *Jane Welsh to Eliza Stodart. La Nouvelle Héloïse.*—George Rennie's last visit.—Reading German with Mr. Carlyle.—A story promised.—A postscript	37
VIII.	Mar. 3 [1822]. From Haddington. *Jane Welsh to Eliza Stodart.* The story of a literary proposal.—Stormy weather.—Thoughts of George Rennie.—Shopping commissions.—News of Irving and Carlyle	44

LETTER		PAGE
IX.	July 22 [1822 or 23?]. From Templand. *Jane Welsh to Eliza Stodart.* A dull time in Dumfriesshire.—Boreland in wet weather.—Sees Benjamin B——, but—on the wrong side of the river.—Irving's triumph in London	60
X.	[Jan., 1823.] From Haddington. *Jane Welsh to Eliza Stodart.* Unwelcome Visitors.—Shandy's reception of the town dog.—Changed opinion of her uncle.—A visit to Edinburgh *in prospectu.*—The binding of Cicero.—A plagiarist of Tom Moore	67
XI.	March, 1823. From Haddington. *Jane Welsh to Eliza Stodart.* A foolish but graceful admirer.—Dulness tempered by Carlyle's letters.—A *genius* found, and—found out.—An Irish packman.—Looking forward to a visit to Edinburgh.—George Rennie	76
XII.	April 18 [1824?]. From Haddington. *Jane Welsh to Eliza Stodart. The* Miss Welsh.—Thomas Carlyle has left Moray Street for the country.—Mother ill.—The man of medicine.—George Rennie.—"Get me a 'jemmy' hat"	83
XIII.	Sept. 27, 1824. From Templand. *Jane Welsh to Eliza Stodart.* James Baillie has all good qualities except genius.—Disillusioned about Benjamin B——.—A pleasant time in the country.—The gossip of a "man from Edinburgh"	90
XIV.	Jan. 18 [1825?]. From Haddington. *Jane Welsh to Eliza Stodart.* A visit from Dugald G——.—Letter from James Baillie about his affairs, and from Carlyle, with autographs of Goethe and Byron.—A cake from Templand.—Music wanted	98
XV.	April 11, 1825. From Haddington. *Jane Welsh to Eliza Stodart.* A visit from Benjamin B——.—Mr. Carlyle and the tea-kettle.—Music wanted	106
XVI.	Aug. 13, 1825. From Templand. *Jane Welsh to Eliza Stodart.* Alternately ill and at parties.—James Baillie's *affairs.*—Going to Annandale	112
XVII.	Sept., 1826. From Templand. *Jane Welsh to Eliza Stodart.* Marriage and marriage presents	116

LETTER			PAGE
XVIII.	Feb. 17, 1827. From 21 Comely Bank, Edinburgh. *Thomas Carlyle to David Aitken.* Enclosing a Testimonial	. . . .	120
XIX.	June 29 [1827]. From 21 Comely Bank, Edinburgh. *Thomas Carlyle to David Aitken.* A parcel from Goethe	. . .	124
XX.	July, 1828. From Craigenputtoch. *Mrs. Carlyle to Eliza Stodart.* Commissions.—Life at Craigenputtoch	. . . .	127
XXI.	[Oct., 1828.] From Craigenputtoch. *Mrs. Carlyle to Eliza Stodart.* Sending money by Mrs. Jeffrey	. . . . .	133
XXII.	Nov. 21, 1828. From Craigenputtoch. *Mrs. Carlyle to Eliza Stodart.* Alone in the moors.—Feeding poultry, but not farming.—Visitors in the autumn.—Learning Spanish.—Perhaps coming to Edinburgh.—Carlyle's sister ill	. . . . .	135
XXIII.	Dec., 1828. From Craigenputtoch. *Mrs. Carlyle to Eliza Stodart.* Prelude to commissions.—A connoisseur in paper.—A brown coffee-pot to replace the broken one.—About packing	. . .	142
XXIV.	Nov. 11, 1829. From Craigenputtoch. *Mrs. Carlyle to Eliza Stodart.* Back from Edinburgh to the desert.—Happy in both.—Visit of George Moir.—Portrait of Mr. Donaldson	. . . . . .	148
XXV.	Dec. 21, 1829. From Craigenputtoch. *Thomas Carlyle to David Aitken.* Projected *History of German Literature.*—Borrowing books.—Winter at Craigenputtoch.—Dr. Carlyle.—Sir W. Hamilton.—Dr. Brewster	. . . . . .	154
XXVI.	Jan. 26, 1830. From Craigenputtoch. *Thomas Carlyle to David Aitken.* Books connected with *History of German Literature.*—"Come and see Craigenputtoch in summer"	. . . . . .	161
XXVII.	Feb. 5 [1830]. From Craigenputtoch. *Mrs. Carlyle to Eliza Stodart.* Death of a pig and other disasters.—A carrier's mistake.—Craigenputtoch in snow		168
XXVIII.	[Dec., 1830, or Jan., 1831?] From Craigenputtoch. *Mrs. Carlyle to Eliza Stodart.* Recovering from a sore throat.—Winter solitude	. . . . . .	173
XXIX.	Jan. 16 [1831?]. From Craigenputtoch. *Mrs.*		

xvi *Contents.*

LETTER		PAGE
	Carlyle to Eliza Stodart. The late political changes. — Digression on a rare moth.—An Irish packman's compliment.—Old Esther of Carstamin . . .	177
XXX.	April, 1831. From Craigenputtoch. *Mrs. Carlyle to Eliza Stodart.* A MS. for Cochrane.—A spring morning.—A flighty goose and a steadfast turkey.—A visitor from Haddington. — A tale of a nettle. P.S. *From Thomas Carlyle to Mr. Bradfute.* On cigars.—An invitation seconded by Mrs. Carlyle	185
XXXI.	June 28, 1831. From Craigenputtoch. *Thomas Carlyle to Sam. Aitken.* About Mr. David Aitken's candidature for a Church History chair.—Probably going to London .	193
XXXII.	Oct., 1832. From Craigenputtoch. *Mrs. Carlyle to Eliza Stodart.*—On the duty of keeping up a correspondence. — "The remains of a fine woman."—Wanted a house in Edinburgh for the winter.—Sober enough now.—Cholera in Dumfries	197
XXXIII.	[Oct. or Nov., 1832.] From Craigenputtoch. *Mrs. Carlyle to Eliza Stodart.* A present of pheasants. — Her mother's illness.—About the Edinburgh house . . .	206
XXXIV.	Dec., 1832. From Craigenputtoch. *Mrs. Carlyle to Eliza Stodart.* After her grandfather's death.—About the Edinburgh house.—Her mother's plans . .	210
XXXV.	Dec., 1832. From Templand. *Mrs. Carlyle to Eliza Stodart.* About the house in Edinburgh	216
XXXVI.	Dec. 22, 1832. From Templand. *Thomas Carlyle to Eliza Stodart.* About the house in Edinburgh	221
XXXVII.	Dec. 26, 1832. From Craigenputtoch. *Thomas Carlyle to Eliza Stodart.* About the house in Edinburgh	223
XXXVIII.	[Mar., 1833.] From 18 Carlton Street, Edinburgh. *Mrs. Carlyle to Eliza Stodart.* The flight of Sapio the singer and its consequences. — A disreputable neighbour.—Ill for two days.—Bidding for an easy chair.—Jeffrey's opinion of Harriet Martineau	227
XXXIX.	May 24, 1833. From Craigenputtoch. *Mrs. Carlyle to Eliza Stodart.* Missed the	

LETTER		PAGE
	coach.—Influenza.—Back at Craigenputtoch.—Burning of a wood	233
XL.	July 28, 1833. From Craigenputtoch.—*Mrs. Carlyle to Eliza Stodart.* Better health.—Needlework and cheesemaking.—Dr. J. Carlyle.— Perhaps going abroad next summer.—Looking back on last winter in Edinburgh	240
XLI.	Nov., 1833. From Craigenputtoch. *Mrs. Carlyle to Eliza Stodart.* A framemaker's excellent memory.—The Moffat expedition.—Bad health traced back to 1817.—Crumbs from Carlyle's table.—The Barjarg library.—Books borrowed from it. — Millinery and dressmaking. — On writing and handwriting	246
XLII.	Jan., 1834. From Craigenputtoch. *Mrs. Carlyle to Eliza Stodart.* A vehement remonstrance	254
XLIII.	July 29, 1834. From 5 Cheyne Row, Chelsea. *Thomas Carlyle to John Bradfute.* The house in Chelsea.—State of literature.—Writing *The French Revolution.*—Death of Coleridge.—Celebrated literary women	256
XLIV.	[1834.] From Chelsea. *Mrs. Carlyle to Eliza Stodart.* How to knit up a ravelled correspondence. — Settled in London.—Noise after the silence of Craigenputtoch.—Better health.—The house in Chelsea.—Neighbours, Leigh Hunt and others.—George Rennie again.—London friends.—An affectionate reception	262
XLV.	Feb., 1836. From Chelsea. *Mrs. Carlyle to Eliza Stodart.* Friendships in youth and middle age.—Recollections of childhood.—London friends: the Sterlings, Pepoli, the Countess Degli Antoni.—An invitation	273
XLVI.	Mar., 1837. From Chelsea. *Mrs. Carlyle to Mrs. Aitken.* Influenza.—Carlyle's Lectures on German Literature. The charm of London life. — Harriet Martineau.—Fanny Kemble.—No idle condolences	282
XLVII.	Sept. 8, 1840. From Chelsea. *Thomas Carlyle to David Aitken.* Peterkin's *Booke of the Universall Kirk*	290
XLVIII.	Dec. 9, 1840. From Chelsea. *Thomas Carlyle to David Aitken.* Baillie's *Letters* wanted.—Book-borrowing.—Books about	

LETTER		PAGE
	Scotch Covenanting.—Mark Napier's *Montrose.*—Young D——.	292
XLIX.	Feb. 22, 1841. From Chelsea. *Thomas Carlyle to David Aitken.* Baillie's *Letters.*—Young D——	297
L.	[Soon after March 30, 1841.] From Chelsea. *Mrs. Carlyle to Mrs. Aitken.* Mr. D——'s enthusiastic letter.—George Rennie.—Curing a sore throat.—Mr. Carlyle, *Passenger to* ——?	300
LI.	[Spring of 1841.] From Chelsea. *Mrs. Carlyle to Miss Scot.* Influenza.—G. Ruffini and Mazzini.—Tried between "fierce extremes."—Old Haddington friends.—Mr. *Keppenwitch.*—A. Ruffini's letter.—Intended visit to Haddington.—Erasmus Darwin and his carriage	303
LII.	May 11 [1847 ?]. From Chelsea. *Mrs. Carlyle to R. Scot Skirving.* An aching head.—How to get to Chelsea.—"Dissolving views."—Thoughts of East Lothian	311
	[Mr. Skirving's reminiscences of the Carlyles 303,	315]
LIII.	June. 1842. From Chelsea. *Mrs. Carlyle to Mrs. Aitken.* Her mother's death.—The journey to Liverpool.—A changed Scotland	317
LIV.	[Late in 1858.] From Chelsea. *Mrs. Carlyle to Mrs. Pringle.* Lord Ashburton's picture.—A cold in consequence.—No pleasure without pain.—A story of her childhood	322
LV.	March 15 [1866]. From Chelsea. *Mrs. Carlyle to David Aitken.* Acknowledging invitation.—Mr. Carlyle going to stay with Mr. Erskine	326

LIST OF ILLUSTRATIONS.

SILHOUETTE OF JANE WELSH	*Frontispiece*	
DR. WELSH'S HOUSE AT HADDINGTON, THE HOME OF JANE WELSH	*To face page*	1
SEALS USED BY JANE WELSH (1-3)	,, ,,	18
FACSIMILE OF PART OF LETTER VI.	,, ,,	34
SEALS USED BY JANE WELSH (4-6)	,, ,,	119
SEALS USED BY CARLYLE AND HIS WIFE (7-9) . .	,, ,,	192
FACSIMILE OF PART OF LETTER XLV. . . .	,, ,,	275
THE RUINED CHANCEL OF HADDINGTON CHURCH, WITH THE GRAVE OF DR. WELSH AND MRS. CARLYLE .	,, ,,	329

I.

[This and the following letter must belong to the autumn of 1819, when Jane Welsh was between eighteen and nineteen years of age. Her father, Dr. Welsh, died in September, 1819. See Carlyle, *Reminiscences*, ed. Froude, ii., p. 94; ed. Norton, i., p. 74; Froude, *Thomas Carlyle*, A. i., p. 115.]

[*No address preserved.—To Miss Eliza Stodart.*]

MY DEAR BESS,—

I think I may say that my mother is a good deal better since I last wrote to you. She still sleeps very badly at night, but she generally has a sound sleep after breakfast. Her appetite is considerably improved; for two or three days she has been almost entirely free of sickness. To-day however she vomited a great deal of bile, but that might proceed from the exertion she made yesterday. We were at church yesterday, the first time we have been out. Oh, how changed everything appeared! We went in a carriage, as my mother would not have been able to have walked; the very sight of the street was hateful to me. I only looked out once, when I thought we were going to stop, and I thought the stones seemed covered with snow, everything looked so white and bleak. We were all three once more under the same roof, and this [is] all that I can ever hope for in this world. No, there is something more. I will one day (and perhaps that day may not be far off) be in the same grave. I have no wish to live, except for two purposes—to be a comfort to my poor mother, and to make myself worthy of being reunited to my adored father. To my many kind relations and friends I am not ungrateful, I love them dearly: but I confess I would with pleasure submit to be separated from them *for a time*, as that separation is to restore me to him; for he was dearer to me than the whole world. I will never cease to be grateful for the sympathy and kindness which we have met with. Among those who will always hold the highest place in my regard I must rank Mrs. Lorimer. The affectionate interest in us which she has displayed, and the sincere distress which *his* loss has occasioned her, have endeared her to me beyond measure. She is very much with us. She would not allow us to go alone yesterday, and it was well we had some one to support us through such an exertion. Her husband,[1] who has also been *exceedingly* kind, preached a most excellent sermon *on that subject* which he knew to be the only one that could excite our interest at such a moment.

I have never heard from Robert[2] yet, so I am still ignorant at what time we may visit Dumfriesshire. I hope to hear from you soon. Excuse this hurried scrawl. With kindest love to your uncle, believe me your affectionate friend.

[*No Signature.*]

---

[1] Rev. Robert Lorimer, one of the two ministers of the parish of Haddington from 1796 till he "went out" in the Disruption of 1843.

[2] Her uncle. See Letter IV., p. 16.

II.

[*No address preserved.—To Miss Eliza Stodart.*]

Sunday Night.

MY DEAR BESS,—

I am happy to say that my mother is no worse than when you left us in her bodily health; for her spirits I cannot say much.

The dreadful loss which we have sustained is one which can never be less deeply felt. Indeed time seems only to show it in more distressing colours. We are all exceedingly obliged to you for your kindness in coming to us at such a time; but we still cannot help thinking that you have some other reason than the one you gave us for leaving us so soon. Both my mother and self are perfectly unconscious of having offended you. Had we had the smallest idea that such was your intention, it would have been the last thing we would have thought of to ask you to go to Edinburgh on our business, or at least to return for so very short a period. I do not think that we can possibly be in Dumfriesshire for three or four weeks from this date, nor do I expect to be in town before that time. Indeed, it is astonishing how little desire I feel to leave this place, even for a short time. The memory of what has been, and the melancholy pleasure in the reflection that I am still near the being that I loved more than all the world besides, although he is no longer conscious of my affection, are the feelings which constitute the little happiness I now can feel. When you was[1] here I did not know that he was buried in the ruin of the church.[2] I cannot tell you how it pleased me. Last night, when the moon was shining so brightly, I felt the most anxious wish to visit his grave; and I will not feel satisfied till I have done so. Those ruins appear to me now to possess a sublimity

---

[1] "Were" was originally written, and then "was" substituted for it.

[2] Cf. the beautiful account of her visit to her father's grave in 1849 in *Letters and Memorials of Jane Welsh Carlyle*, ii., p. 59 ff. The choir of Haddington church is in ruins, the nave being used as the present parish church.

with which my fancy never before vested them. I feel that I never can leave this place. May God bless you, and preserve you from such a loss as mine, is the prayer of

Your affectionate Friend,
JANE WELSH.

III.

[The position assigned to Letters III. and V. is purely conjectural. There is nothing by which I can definitely fix the dates. I have adopted the order that seemed most plausible and most convenient to the reader.]

To Miss Stodart, 22 George Square, Edinburgh.

[Early in 1820?]

MY DEAR BESS,—

This is not intended to be a letter of friendship, but merely one to give trouble. My Aunt Elizabeth is seized with a wondrous passion to grow clever—or, perhaps I ought to say, to be accomplished. She has commenced drawing, French, and geography under my auspices. As she has no drawing materials, I must request that you will take the trouble to get from White a paint-box (I think they come to about twelve shillings) containing the usual number of paints, only, instead of light blue and light green, I would like a small cake of carmine, and a cake of king's yellow; also a few hair brushes of different sizes, and four small sheets of *thin*, white pasteboard (I think it is called Bristol sheet), for painting *single* flowers on. For myself I would thank you to get a small cake of carmine, two *very fine* hair brushes, and the same number of sheets of *small*, thin pasteboard. Be so good as cause him to make the *note distinct*, that is to say separate (as the young lady is *particularly particular*). To be done with my commissions at once, I would also thank you to send my Mother black feathers. I will send my buff one to be dyed black the first opportunity. I have been very busy for some time past with Italian, French, etc., etc. Tell Mr. Aitken[1] that I am quite pleased with the Testament. Besides *myself* I have got three pupils, Elizabeth, Ellen Howden, and her cousin Christina. The first is *clever*, but much too

---

[1] *Qu.* Sam Aitken or David Aitken? I think the "Mr." proves it to be the former, as "David Aitken" does not receive that title in the earlier letters. See *Pref.*, p. viii.

confident in her own powers; the second is *exceedingly* clever, but careless; the third is stupid and anxious, and, what is worst, I am more anxious about her than any of them. She is my pupil for everything, and lives with us. Her father and mother died within three months; and when we invited her here, it gave me a melancholy pleasure to think that the care and anxiety which my adored father spent on my education might be of use to one, like me, left destitute of this first blessing. Her father was ill *four days*, and died on the *Sunday* before that fatal one which blasted all my prospects of happiness in this world. She too was going to Mrs. Seaton's[2]; and she was thus, before I saw her, connected to me by the strongest of all possible ties—sympathy. She is beautiful, and very interesting—about fourteen years of age; fortunately for herself she is either not come

---

[2] Haddington correspondents tell me that a widow lady, Mrs. Seton, kept a girls' boarding-school at Ballincrieff House, near Aberlady, and afterwards at Seton House (on the site of the ancient palace), not far from Prestonpans.

to the age in which one feels keenly, or is not naturally endowed with very keen feelings. I confess I am a little disappointed in this respect; but it is wrong in me to be so, for it is certainly a blessing to the poor child.

He used always to tell me that in giving me a good education he was leaving me the greatest good. Of this I have found the truth, and too late I have begun to feel towards him gratitude, which only adds to my sorrow for having it no longer in my power to make any returns. The habits of study in which I have been brought up have done much to support me. I never allow myself to be one moment unoccupied. I read the books he wished me to understand. I have engaged in the plan of study he wished me to pursue; and to the last moment of my life it shall be my endeavour to act in all things exactly as he would have desired. When I am giving his sister and Christina their lessons, I seem to be filling his place; and the recollection of his anxiety and kindness and unwearied exertions for my improvement and for the improvement of those who have so soon forgot him is sometimes like to break my heart.[3]

My Grandfather is a kind old man to come so far at this season. He is very anxious that we should accompany us [? him] to Edinburgh; but to that I am certain my mother will never consent. We have just had a card from John to say that he is coming to tea; I must therefore close this hurried, stupid, troublesome letter. I must beg that you will take the trouble to send out my things as soon as you *conveniently* can, as all my pupils[4] . . . want carmine. Robert arrived to-day, looking divine; I do like him dearly. We had a call yesterday from George B—— and his son Benjamin, who is one of the most frank, unaffected young men I have seen. By the bye Benjamin had a party some

---

[3] "The brave man himself [her father] I never saw: but my poor Jeannie, in her best moments, often said to me, about this or that, 'Yes, *he* would have done it so!' 'Ah, *he* would have liked you!' as her highest praise."—Carlyle, *Reminiscences*, ed. Froude, ii., p. 115; ed. Norton, i., p. 144.

[4] The paper is torn here.

time ago of young doctors from Edinburgh, amongst whom was my old Barkly [5] Museum friend, Mowbray Thomson, who does not seem to have forgot me. He is immensely improved. I dare say you are a little curious to know the state of my *affairs* at present. I must defer all communications till we meet, which I think will be in summer; and indeed you have not much to learn. My *sentiments* and *views* are very much changed, and I believe in time I shall be *really sensible*. Tell Mr. Aitken that I can read two pages of Italian at a time.

Burn this scrawl, I will not say *before you* read it, but immediately after. By the bye you was with me when I told Muir that I wanted the music at different times. He means to make me take 9£ worth of stuff all at once; the thing is quite absurd, and as it will be long, long before I require it, it would really be

---

[5] *Sic.* The museum of human and comparative anatomy formed by John Barclay (d. 1826) now forms part of the collection of the Edinburgh College of Surgeons.

a loss to me. I wish you would go with Robert some day and tell him about it; he has given me a great deal of trouble. I have no room for loves.

Yours affectionately,

JANE B. WELSH.

IV.

To Miss Stodart, 22 George Square, Edinburgh, N.B.

Liverpool,
October 14th, 1820.

My dear Bess,—

You may perhaps remember the name of the person who now address[es] you; more of me, I think, you can scarcely recollect.

I know not how it is that we are such bad correspondents. I believe it is I who am in fault at present; but the shortness of your last must be some excuse for me, for I really expected you would have written to me again, without waiting for an answer to it. But I suspect the real cause of my negligence will be with more justice found in something which I *dare scarcely* name (I mean your *goodnature*): for there are many persons, whom I don't like half so well, whose letters I answer pretty regularly, because I know, were I not to do so, I should never be forgiven;

but from you I always make myself sure of a pardon as soon as I acknowledge my offence. I have now, according to custom, filled my first page with apologies, and so I will proceed to give you some account of our motions. We left Strathmilligan about a fortnight ago, and a sad morning we had of it; but this world is made up of little else than partings. Mr. Robert McTurk, our Landlord's eldest son, drove us in his gig to Dumfries, from whence we posted to Carlisle,[1] and there we took the coach, or rather the coach took us, to Liverpool. Mr. McTurk accompanied us to Penrith, on his way to Brughhill.[2] At Dumfries we drank tea, and slept at Mr. Kirkpatric[k]'s. Roger is a kind, kind man in his

---

[1] She spells it "Carslile" here and at the end of the letter. In her first written communication to Carlyle (June, 1821) she spelt his name in the same way. See Norton, *Early Letters of Thomas Carlyle*, i., p. 354: "Miss Welsh's 'compliments' to Mr. Car*slile*, a gentleman in whom it required no small sagacity to detect my own representative!"

[2] *Sic*. This must be Brough Hill, near Brough, in Westmoreland. A horse and cattle fair is held there annually at the end of September.

own house, and his wife, though not very taking in her appearance, is no less so. Captain Thorburn was there, just the same sentimental-looking person with the open mouth that used to go about catching flies in Edinburgh. My uncle Robert was also there. We had the pleasure of his company for two days at Strathmilligan. It would be rather foolish in me to fill my paper with an eulogium on my own uncle, but I never can resist praising Robert to those who I think place any value on my opinion. His kindness and attention to us merits[3] my warmest gratitude. I have lost my dearest and my best friend, whose love was my most valuable blessing; and the blank he has made to me must be felt till the last moment of my existence, were my life to be much longer than I wish it to be. But *had it been possible* for the loss of such a father to be supplied, it would have been supplied by his brother: but oh! Bess, you knew him, and you know how impossible it is that I should ever

---

[3] *Sic.*

love any human being as I loved him. My
Mother's health, I am glad to say, continues
pretty good, and everybody says she is looking well. We expect to be at Haddington some-
time next month. What a return will it be! no
one to welcome us. When I think of home,
all the pleasure that I feel at the prospect of
seeing so many kind friends again is damped
by that thought. My Uncle[4] and Mary are very
kind, but, between ourselves, I don't like her.
She is certainly a well-principled woman; but
good principles cannot in my opinion make up
for the *total* want of all feminine graces of mind.
She is very fond of argument, and invariably
loses her temper. She is a great politician, which
in a lady is detestable. In fact, she cannot bear
to be contradicted in anything. We have walked
about the town frequently. It is a neat, clean-
looking place. It is much larger than Edinburgh;
but, the houses being all built of brick, there is

---

[4] "Uncle John," her mother's brother. See Carlyle,
Reminiscences, ed. Froude, ii., pp. 142-145; ed. Norton, i.,
pp. 166-168.

nothing at all grand-looking about it. I liked the appearance of Carlisle[5] very much; the castle has a very fine effect. There are some people coming here to tea, so I must close this stupid letter with a promise to be more particular next time. Do write to me soon. My Mother joins me in kindest love to your uncle and yourself.

Yours affectionately,
JANE BAILLIE WELSH.

[*P.S.*]—Address to me to the care of
LEISHMAN & WELSH in Co.,
Red Cross Street,
Liverpool.

---

[5] Cf. *note* 1, p. 15.

SEALS USED BY JANE WELSH.
(Double the Size of the Originals.)

1

Seal used on Letters between 1820 and 1823.

2

A l'Amista, "To Friendship."; Seal used on Letter IV.

3

Seal used on Letters IX., XIII., XVI.—all written from Templand. "J. B. W." most probably means "Jane Baillie Welsh;" but what is "R. K."?

[*Face p.* 18.

V.

To Miss Stodart, 22 George Square, Edinburgh.

HADDINGTON,

8th March [1821 ?].

WELL, my beloved Cousin, here I am once more at the bottom of the pit of dulness, hemmed in all round, straining my eyeballs and stretching my neck to no purpose.

Was ever starling in a more desperate plight?[1] But I *will* "*get out*"—by the wife of Job, I *will!* Here is no sojourn for me. I must dwell in the open world, live amid life; but *here* is no life, no motion, no variety. It is the dimmest, deadest spot (I verily believe) in the Creator's universe;

---

[1] Cf. Letter XLVII., p. 291, where Carlyle says: "Like Sterne's Starling, one has to say mournfully, 'I can't get out!'" The starling comes from the *Sentimental Journey* (vol. ii., p. 24, in edition of 1775).

to look round in it, one might imagine that time had made a stand: the shopkeepers are to be seen standing at the doors of their shops, in the very same postures in which they have stood there ever since I was born. "*The thing that hath been is that also which shall be*"; everything is the *same*, everything is stupid; the very air one breathes is impregnated with stupidity. Alas, my native place! the Goddess of dulness has strewed it with all her poppies!

But it is my native place still! and, after all, there is much in it that I love. I love the bleaching green, where I used to caper and roll, and tumble, and make gowan[2] necklaces, and chains of dandelion stalks, in the days of my "*wee existence*"; and the schoolhouse where I carried away prizes, and signalized myself, not more for the quickness of my parts than for the valour of my arm, above all the boys of the

---

[2] The "gowan" is the daisy. Readers of Dickens will remember how Mr. Micawber was puzzled by the word in *Auld Lang Syne*.

community;[3] and the mill-dam too, where I performed feats of agility which it was easier to extol than to imitate, and which gained me at the time the reputation of a sticket callant[4] (*un garçon assassiné*), which I believe I have maintained with credit up to the present hour; and, above all, I feel an affection for a field by the side of the river, where corn is growing now, and where a hayrick once stood—you remember it?[5] For my part I shall never forget that summer's day; but cherish it "*within the secret cell of the heart*" as long as I live—the sky was so bright, the air so balmy, the whole universe so beautiful! I was very happy then! all my little world lay glittering in tinsel at my feet! But years have passed over it since; and storm after

---

[3] Cf. Carlyle, *Reminiscences*, ed. Froude, ii., p. 73; ed. Norton, i., p. 56; Froude, *Thomas Carlyle*, A. i., pp. 119, 120.

[4] *I.e.* one who has stuck in the process of becoming a lad ("callant" is Fr. *gallant*)—a phrase formed on the analogy of "sticket minister," which a French translator of Scott is said to have turned into "*un ministre assassiné*," a rendering here adapted by Miss Welsh.

[5] Cf. Letter XLV., p. 276.

storm has stripped it of much of its finery. *Allons, ma chère!*—let us talk of the "goosish" man, my quondam lover.⁶

He came; arrived at the George Inn at eleven o'clock at night, twelve hours after he received my answer to his letter; slept there "*more soundly,*" according to his own statement, "*than was to have been expected, all the circumstances of the case considered,*" and in the morning sent a few nonsensical lines to announce his nonsensical arrival. Mother and I received him more politely "than was to have been expected, all the circumstances of the case considered"; and we proceeded to walk, and play at battledoor, and talk inanities, about new novels, and new belles, and what had gone on at a splendid party the night before, where he had been (he told us) for half an hour *with his arm under his hat;* and

---

⁶ Which of them? Is this "Dugald G——" (cf. pp. 96, 99)? or is it "John W——" (cf. p. 76)? or is it rather a third person, a Mr. A—— (to whom the remark, "All the circumstances," etc., is ascribed on p. 99)? or is it some one else?

then he corrected himself, and said, *with his head under his arm!* It was of very little consequence where his head was; it is not much worth; but the Lord defend me from visitors so equipped, when I come to give parties! Before dinner he retired to his Inn, and vapoured back, in the course of an hour or so, in all the pride of two waistcoats (one of figured velvet, another of sky-blue satin), gossamer silk stockings, and morocco leather slippers—"*these little things are great to little men.*"[7] I should not like to pay his tailor's bill however. Craigenputtock[8] could not stand

---

[7] Carlyle, writing to his brother Alexander in 1831 about the difficulty of getting a farm, says, "Little things are great to little men, to little man" (Froude, *Thomas Carlyle*, A. ii., p. 143)—a less remote application of the line (from Goldsmith's *Traveller*), "These little things are great to little man."

[8] She here spells Craigenputtock (which was now her own property) with a *ck*. In all the rest of these letters it seems (when written in full) to be invariably spelt with a *ch*. Did Carlyle ultimately prefer the spelling *ck* (which is adopted by Mr. Froude, except in his edition of the *Reminiscences*, and by Prof. Norton) because of the etymological connexion with "puttock," a hawk? See passage from *Reminiscences* quoted in *note* on Letter XXXIX., p. 237.

it. Next morning he took himself away, leaving us more impressed with the idea of his imbecility than ever. In a day or two after his return to town, there came a huge parcel from him, containing a letter for Mother expressed with a still greater command of absurdity than any of the preceding ones, and a quantity of music for me (*pour parenthèse*, I shall send you a sheet of it, having another copy of "Home, Sweet Home," beside), and in two days more another letter, and another supply of music. Hitherto there had been nothing of *hope*, nothing more of love or marrying; but now my gentleman presumed to flatter himself, in the expansion of the folly of his heart, that *I might possibly change my mind.* Ass! I change my mind, indeed! and for him! Upon my word, to be an imbecile as he is, he has a monstrous stock of modest assurance! However I very speedily relieved him of any doubts which he might have upon the matter. I told him "*ce que j'ai fait je le ferois encore,*" in so many words as must (I think) have brought him to his senses—if he has any. He has since written to Mother, begging of her to deprecate my displeasure. There the transaction rests, and peace be with us!

I have neither heard nor seen anything of "Doctor Fieff"[9]—the Lord be praised! He not only wasted a very unreasonable proportion of my time, but his *fuffs* and explosions were very hurtful to my nervous system.

Talking of nerves, we got a horrible fright in church on Saturday. An old lady dropt down in the adjoining seat, and was carried out as dead. Mother screamed out "Oh" so stoutly, that Mr. Gordon was obliged to stop in his prayer, and sit down. She seems destined to make a distinguished figure in all church hubbubs. Witness the scene of the repenting-stool. The old lady has got better.

What of *Wull?* is he coming out soon? A visit from any man with brains in his head would really be an act of mercy to us here.

---

[9] Dr. Fyffe. Carlyle spells it "Fyfe." See *Reminiscences*, ed. Froude, ii., p. 93; ed. Norton, i., p. 70.

There is a long letter for you! Now will you write to me soon? I cannot recollect your excuse without some feeling of displeasure—" *You cannot write letters that I will care about.*" Surely this compliment to my understanding (if it was meant as such) is at the expense of my heart. It is not for the sake of grammar or rhetorick (I should think) that friends, like you and I, write to one another. When your letters cease to interest me, credit me, I will not ask them.

My mother has quite got rid of her cold. It was as bad as need be after we came home. For myself I am quite well, still suffering a little from the *maladie des adieux;* but that is all.

Both of us unite in kindest love to your Uncle and yourself. Will you kiss him for me?

Ever most affectionately yours,

JANE BAILLIE WELSH.

[*P.S.*] Mother bids me say that all the difference betwixt your manner of making marmalade and hers is, that she gives double the quantity of sugar to the fruit. If you think however that she has any art in it which you are not up to, she will be exceedingly happy to make it for you. Speaking of marmalade, will you give my compliments to William Watson?

Mother is never to be done with bidding me say. She bids me say next that Betty's[10] Mama's hens stand very much in need of pills. However she means to look about on Monday (there's one of my old blunders) to see if the hens are more laxative in another quarter—how dirty!

Will you put the note and the letter into the post office? The Lord give me patience! Mother bids me say again that there is abundance of fruit and sugar to be had here, so that if she is to have the pleasure of making the

---

[10] The old servant, I suppose, frequently referred to in *Letters and Memorials;* e.g. ii., p. 78.

marmalade for Bradie, you need not send any. *Moreover*—oh—she has plenty of cursed ugly wee black pigs[11] at your service. Not one word more will I write for her, by God!

---

[11] *I.e.* earthenware jars—to put the marmalade in. This Scotch word "pig" has been a fruitful source of mystery to unaccustomed Southerners.

VI.

[Carlyle was introduced to Miss Welsh by Edward Irving in the end of May, 1821. It may have been Carlyle who first induced her to read Rousseau (see letter of Irving in Froude, *Thomas Carlyle*, i., p. 135). In another letter (*ib.*, p. 155) Irving may *possibly* be referring to *La Nouvelle Héloïse* under the name "Rousseau's Letters." This letter must be later than July 14th, 1821; and, as the two following letters must come at no very great interval, and as Letter VIII. is dated "March," this one probably belongs to the end of 1821 or beginning of 1822.]

To Miss Stodart.

HADDINGTON.

MY DEAR BESS,—

I returned the two first volumes of *Julia*,[1] with many thanks. It seems to me, that the most proper way of testifying my gratitude to the amiable Jean Jacques for the pleasure he has afforded me is to do what in me lies to extend the circle of his admirers. I shall begin

---

[1] I.e. *La Nouvelle Héloïse*, of which Julie Étange is the heroine.

with you. Do read this book. You will find it tedious in many of its details, and in some of its scenes culpably indelicate; but for splendour of eloquence, refinement of sensibility, and ardour of passion it has no match in the French language. Fear not that by reading *Héloïse* you will be ruined, or undone, or whatever adjective best suits that fallen state into which women and angels *will* stumble *at a time*. I promise you that you will rise from the *Héloïse* with a deeper impression of whatever is most beautiful and most exalted in virtue than is left upon your mind by Blair's Sermons, Paley's Theology, or the voluminous Jeremy Taylor himself.[2] I never felt my mind more prepared to brave temptation of every sort than when I closed the second volume of this strange book. I believe if the Devil himself had waited upon me [in] the shape of Lord Byron,[3] I would have desired Betty to

---

[2] She spells the names "Pailey" and "Tailor." Below she writes "Johnny-groats."

[3] For her intense admiration of Lord Byron, cf. Letter XIV., pp. 101, 102, and *note* 6.

show him out. Sages say that every work which presents vice in the colours of virtue has a tendency to corrupt the morals. They are without doubt in the right; but when they say that *Julia Étange* is vicious, they are in a most egregious mistake. Read the book, and ask your heart, or rather your judgment, if *Julia* be vicious. *I do not wish to countenance such irregularities among my female acquaintances;* but I must confess, were any individual of them to meet with *such a man*, to struggle as she struggled, to endure as she endured, to *yield* as she yielded, and to repent as she repented, I would love that woman better than the chastest, coldest prude between John o' Groat's House and Land's End. One serious bad consequence will result to you from reading *Héloïse*—at least, if your soul-strings are screwed up to the same key as mine. You will never marry! Alas! I told you I should die a virgin, if I reached twenty *in vain*.[4] Even so will it prove. This

---

[4] She was twenty on July 14th, 1821.

Book, this fatal Book, has given me an idea of a love so *pure* (yes, you may laugh! but I repeat it), so pure, so constant, so disinterested, so exalted, that no love the men of this world can offer me will ever fill up the picture my imagination has drawn with the help of Rousseau. No lover will Jane Welsh ever find like St. Preux, no husband like Wolmar (I don't mean to insinuate that *I should like both*); and to no man will she ever give her heart and pretty hand who bears to these no resemblance. George Rennie! James Aitken! Robert MacTurk![5] James Baird!!![6] Robby Angus!—O Lord, O Lord! where is the St. Preux? Where

---

[5] Robert MacTurk is referred to in *Letters and Memorials of Jane Welsh Carlyle*, ii., p. 392, where (in a letter of 1858) she speaks of sending him a present (*qu.* a photograph of "our interior" at Chelsea?) as "a sort of *amende honorable* for having failed to give him myself—Good God! when he had some right to expect it—long ago, when I was an extremely absurd little girl. His good feeling towards me, after all, deserves a certain esteem from me, and a certain recognition, which, I hope, has been put into an acceptable form for him in the peep-show!"

[6] Cf. Letter VIII., p. 46.

is the Wolmar? Bess, I am in earnest—I shall never marry; and, after having laughed so at old maids, it will be so dreadful to be one of the very race at whom I have pointed the finger of scorn. Virtuous, venerable females! how my heart smites me for the ill-judged ridicule I have cast on their pure names! What atonement can I make? What punishment shall I undergo? Let me think! I will—I will write a novel, and make my Heroine a Beauty, a Wit, a very *monster of perfection*, an Empress of a thousand *male* hearts; and—she shall live a Maid, and die in an elegant little garret. But I will talk no more on this melancholy subject. So you saw my Aunt! What did you think of her? Poor thing! she does not understand love. She never read *Héloïse;* but she has got a husband —such as he is.

Mr. Craig Buchanan has put me to the expense of postage[7] twice within the last fort-

---

[7] That is to say, of course, by *sending* letters. Prepayment was unusual in the days before the penny post.

night. He is improving in his style, and displays some ingenuity in finding out subjects to write upon. He threatens me with a visit in a week or two. It will surely come to a crisis: what do you think of it? He is about the age of Wolmar; but Wolmar had not a bald head, nor a lame leg, neither did Wolmar make puns or pay compliments. I have just had a letter from Thomas Carlyle: he too speaks of coming. He is something liker to St. Preux than George Craig is to Wolmar. He has *his* talents, *his* vast and cultivated mind, *his* vivid imagination, *his* independence of soul, and *his* high-souled principles of honour. But then— Ah, these *buts!*—St. Preux never kicked the fire-irons, nor made puddings in his teacup. Want of Elegance! Want of Elegance, Rousseau says, is a defect which no woman can overlook.[8] It is the decree of fate! dear Eliza, it is the decree of fate! so look about for a nice, pleasant,

---

[8] "La privation des graces est un défaut, que les femmes ne pardonnent point."—*La Nouvelle Héloïse*, Part i., Lettre 45. [This reference I owe to Mr. Saintsbury.]

just had a letter from Thomas Carlyle he too speaks of
coming. He is something likes to Aff Bury thou George Gray
is Holmar. He has his talents his vast and cultivated
mind — his vivid imagination — his indpendence of soul
and his own high bold principle of honour. But then
Ah these hats! Affshuns recoils hiltho the pro now — no —
more puddings in his teacup. Taut of Elegance — taut
of Elegance Rousseau says is a object which no woman
can overlook. — It is the dew of fate. Dear Eliza, it is
the dews of fate. So look about for a nice pleasant
little g huiexl that has a fine view overlooks by
the flowers smoke and out of reach of this camera
obscura and we will tothe up house together —

— Shaw!

little garret that has a fine view unclouded by the town smoke and out of reach of the *camera obscura*, and we will take up house together. When I commenced this letter I did not intend to write above three lines; the determined and somewhat unkind manner in which you declared you would carry on no further correspondence with me still sticks in my thrapple.[9] I allow you however an opportunity of mending your manners; take care that you do not abuse it. My Mother sends her kind compliments, and will be glad to hear from you. Love to Brady and Maggy. Send me, if you please, with first opportunity, the third volume of *Julia*.

I have never seen him[10] since I came home.

---

[9] *I.e.* wind-pipe.

[10] George Rennie apparently. " The most serious-looking of these affairs was that of George Rennie, the Junior (not Heir, but *Cadet*) of *Phantassie*, Nephew of the first Engineer Rennie; a clever, decisive, very ambitious, but quite *un*melodious young fellow; whom we knew afterwards here as sculptor, as M.P. (for a while),—finally as retired Governor of the Falkland Islands, in which latter character he died here, seven or eight years ago."—Carlyle, *Reminiscences*, ed. Norton, i., p. 70; ed. Froude, ii., p. 92.

His Mother and Janet called one day, and I saw John at the foxhounds. Oh wretch! I wish I could hate him, but I cannot; I despise him, but I do not hate him; and when Friday comes, I always think how neatly I used to be dressed, and sometimes I give my hair an additional brush and put on a clean frill, just from habit. Oh! the devil take him! he has wasted all the affections of my poor heart, and now there is not a vestige of a flirt about me: but I will vex that renegade heart of his yet.

[*No Signature.*]

VII.

To Miss Stodart, 22 George Square.

[Early in 1822.]

MY DEAR ELIZA,—

I thank you for your letter, which gave me much pleasure, and would have given me still more, had it wanted the professions of humility at the beginning. Once for all, Miss Eliza Stodart, I give you to understand that sincerity is my favourite virtue. You know whether it could be consistent with sincerity to ask—nay, urge a person to write to me whose letters afford me neither pleasure nor amusement. I have finished *Julia*—divine Julia! What a finished picture of the most sublime virtue! If ever I have a child (which God forbid! my resolutions against matrimony holding out) she shall "read it by day, and meditate by night." If ever I am rich enough to furnish a library, it shall be the first book I buy, and shall occupy the same shelf with Chalmers and my Bible.

This is no joking. *Julia* is decidedly the most moral book I ever read. We quite mistook its nature formerly. In the second and third volumes there is not one word that the most squeamish woman could be ashamed of. Julia never *relapses!* To the last hour, last minute of her life, she is pure and bright, as the silver moon when the dark cloud that obscured it for a moment has passed away. Oh, she is a glorious creature!—is? would to God she really *was!* I would travel far to see her! I would never leave her 'till she vowed to be my friend. But, alas! she is a vision! like everything *perfectly* glorious and beautiful, she is a vision!

But back to beings of this world! George Rennie—read, wonder, but be silent—George Rennie is on the sea! and will soon be in Italy! What does he seek there? you will ask. His friends answer, "Improvement in the art of sculpture." I answer—"Ruin." Yes! the die is cast —his fate is decided! This liberty, this fatal liberty, that his too indulgent Father allows him can lead only to ruin. False, heartless as he is,

I tremble to think on all the dangers, the allurements to which he is about to be exposed—and in such a frame of mind! How little fit to offer any resistance! It is some weeks ago since Nancy Wilkie told my Mother that he meditated going abroad for the purpose of improving his taste in this stucco business, which it seems, he means to prosecute *as a profession.* Chantry and Joseph have cruelly told him he has a genius for it; and who is unwilling to believe himself a genius? This report was afterwards confirmed by Dr. Thomson, who had been at Phantassie, and told us he thought of inviting Benjamin by a Dr. Quin or George Rennie, who was to leave Phantassie on the Saturday following. Can you believe it? this intelligence afflicted me. We had not seen each other for months, and yet it seemed that we were now for the first time to be quite parted. I had not heard his voice for many a day; but then I had heard those who had conversed with him, I had seen objects he had looked on, I had breathed the air that he had breathed. But now seas and countries were to lie betwixt us. The sun and the moon were to be the only objects we could behold in common. *This* looked like *separation!* Yet do not blame me or think me weak: it was the recollection of the past that made me weep at his departure, and not the pain of the present. I supped at the Davidsons' that night; James Wilkie told me he had called with George at our house some days before! but found us out. I had not heard of this. My mother had concealed it from me. What did she fear? absurd! Next day was the day preceding his departure. I resolved to return him his letters, lest I might *never* have another opportunity, and I seemed to keep them like a sword over his head. I sealed them, and scarcely had finished when I heard a rap. I knew it at once; long, long I had not heard it, and yet I recognised it in an instant to be his. I ran out of the room. On the stairs I met Janet Ewart, who was staying here. She is very nervous, and thought proper to utter a loud scream. "I looked so pale," she said; "she took me for a ghost"! Idiot! You may suppose such a folly, which must have had a most strange appearance to him (for he could not but hear the scream), was not calculated to restore my composure. I told her that the hurry in which I had run out of the room to change my shoes had made me sick; but I added as resolutely as a Roman, "As I hear it is *only* George Rennie, we may go down." Down we accordingly went. He half advanced to shake hands with me; I made him a cold bow. He placed a chair for me, and went on conversing with my Mother. He looked well—handsome—quite in high health and seemingly in high spirits. I scarcely heard a word he said, my own heart beat so loud. At length he rose. He took leave of my mother; then looked at me as if uncertain what to do. I held out my hand; he took it, and said "Good-bye!" I answered him, "*Farewell.*" He left the house! Such was the concluding scene of our *Romance!* Great God! he left the house—the *very room* where—no matter—as if he had never been in it in his life before—unfeeling wretch! It was a dreadful trial to me to be obliged to save appearances even for some minutes *after* he was gone; but I went through it bravely! I returned his letters that night with a note (on account of which you would have blushed for me), so that he might receive them just immediately before his setting out, which would effectually prevent any reply: and now am I done with him *for ever.*

Mr. Buchanan has not yet been here. I forgot to answer his letters. No wonder he has not come, when I never said he would be welcome. Mr. Carlyle was with us two days, during the greater part of which I read German with him. It is a noble language! I am getting on famously. He scratched the fender dreadfully. I must have a pair of carpet-shoes and handcuffs prepared for him the next time. His tongue only should be left at liberty: his other members are most fantastically awkward.

A very laughable thing happened to me lately; but as my fingers are cramped with writing so long, I will delay the recital till another time. If you have any curiosity (and what woman is without?) you will write me forthwith, for you shall not have this good story till you *ask it.*

Kindest love to Maggy and your Uncle. She and you have quite mistaken my character, since you laugh at my chaste views. I will be happier contemplating my "*beau idéal*" than a *real, substantial,* eating, drinking, sleeping, *honest* husband. My mother joins my kind wishes for you all.

Your affectionate friend,
JANE BAIL[1]

They say a postscript is the most important part of a lady's letter.[2] If this be a general maxim, I need not make an apology for writing what I am about to say *outside my letter.* My Mother and I anxiously desire—hope—expect—that you and Maggy will come out for a week or so before she leaves town. She has never been here yet, and it will be very unkind in you if you do not bring her.

---

[1] The signature is unfinished.
[2] Cf. Edith Bellenden's letter in *Old Mortality*, chap. x.

VIII.

[*No address preserved.—To Miss Eliza Stodart.*]

HADDINGTON,

3rd March [1822].

MY DEAR ELIZA,—

You have paid the price of my story, so you shall have it, though I fear that, like other good things, it will lose sadly in the telling.

Some days before I last wrote to you, I received a letter, addressed to me in a copper-plate hand, folded with mathematical exactness, and sealed with the most scrupulous nicety. As the hand was new to me, I turned the letter round and round, and thought on every possible quarter whence it could have come, till at length it *struck me all of a heap* that by breaking the seal I might penetrate into the interior and satisfy my curiosity. Within an *envelope* I found the following card:

"Mr. George — Cunningham presents his most

respectful compliments to Miss Welsh, and will do himself the honour of waiting upon her, at any time she may appoint, for the purpose of holding some conversation respecting a projected literary work, in which the young lady's assistance would be peculiarly useful."

This billet puzzled me exceedingly, its writer being a person with whom I was not even on bowing terms. Mr. George Cunningham[1] is an orphan, who has been brought up in Haddington with his uncle, Mr. Ainsley—a good-looking man without an arm, who sits in the chapel,[2] has a

---

[1] If this be the "George Cunningham" mentioned in the account of her visit to Haddington in 1849 (*Letters and Memorials*, ii., p. 73)—"the boy of our school who never got into trouble, and never helped others out of it"—she must at that time have forgotten all about *this* interview; for she there says she had seen him once since school days, "at Craik's, some twelve years ago." Mr. William Ainsley is referred to on the same page as some one she did not know, or at least recollect having known.

[2] *I.e.* (I suppose) is an Episcopalian, as distinct from a frequenter of the parish church or of a Seceder " meeting-house." In *Letters and Memorials*, ii., p. 316, is a reference to " the chapel " at Haddington.

bald head that shines like glass, lives very retiredly, and once poisoned all Mrs. Cunningham the thread-woman's hens, for which misdemeanour he was fined twenty pounds to the School of Industry. The said George was, when a very young boy, in the mathematical class with me; but during the latter part of his existence, which has (I understand) been spent in Mr. Davidson's office, he had quite worn out of my acquaintance, and almost out of my recollection. After various musings I came to this decision, that the Creature (who was really clever at school, and won a prize from me) had written some mathematical work for which he wanted subscribers, and thought to engage my interest by submitting his labours to my criticism; or else, said the imp of vanity within (not to be silenced, it would seem, by the most humiliating rebuffs), or else he has, like James Baird, fallen in love with me from *hearsay*, and takes this extraordinary method of getting himself introduced into my presence. The card however required an answer, so I forthwith wrote:

"Miss Welsh will be *at home* all this evening, and glad to hear from Mr. Cunningham of any project which may, in its results, prove advantageous to an old school-fellow, though she is greatly at a loss to conjecture what assistance towards any 'literary work' can lie with her, an individual utterly unknown in the Literary world, and little qualified to attain any distinction there."

This last clause was put in merely for modesty's sake, for even then I was planning the *immortalizing of old maids*.[3]

After sitting in expectation for some hours (my Mother ever and anon repeating that I was really a *very great character*), it came into my head that the card was probably a quiz written by some of his companions. My Mother and I fell into fits of laughter at the idea of the effect my answer would produce upon the poor lad if he was unconscious of having said or written anything to call it forth; and just when our mirth was at the loudest the door opened, and the said George, *in*

---

[3] Cf. p. 33.

propriâ personâ, stood before us. The terrible agitation visible in his deportment at his entrance strengthened my suspicions of his heart. I held out my hand to him with a *most winning smile* of condescension, but *even* MY smile did not restore him to composure. He seated himself with his eyes most religiously fixed upon the carpet, and there was silence. My Mother vouchsafed a remark upon the weather; the unfortunate Creature replied in a quavering voice, and again there was silence. At length my Mother, compassionating the deplorable stagnation of his intellect, withdrew. The door closed on us. The literary man looked into the fire, and I looked at the literary man; and a queer, little, odd-shaped man it was. He coughed sundry times, and at length began:

"You, no doubt, expect, MADAM, that I am going to produce a novel or tragedy of my own composition for your perusal, but—but really I have no such thing."

So! (thought I) it is as I suspected. This odd Thing is really in love with me!

"The subject," he continued, "which I wish to mention to you is—it is—a Magazine."

The last word came out of his throat bolt, as if a bullet had been at its back, and the Creature seemed much relieved.

"A Magazine?" I repeated with surprise, the intelligence conveyed by this important word not being so luminous as he seemed to have anticipated. "A Magazine here—in Haddington? Do you mean to write a Magazine?"

"I mean to assist," he replied somewhat peevishly; "and I am of opinion that this county affords local interest sufficient to render a work of that sort, published by Mr. Tait, extremely acceptable. All that is wanting *is people to write it.*" (What a desideratum!!)

"I do not doubt," I replied, "if you can find people to write it, and people to read it, *Tait's Magazine* will do just as well as *Blackwood's* or *Waugh's*,[4] or anybody else's."

---

[4] Waugh, an Edinburgh bookseller, was the publisher of the *New Edinburgh Review*, which died before the end of 1823. Carlyle contributed an article on Joanna Baillie's

"If you and those who are *qualified* would only *step forward*," said *the George*.

"But really, sir, I *do not* feel myself qualified to engage in such an undertaking."

"Ah! Miss Welsh," exclaimed the Creature, growing very bold, "you must not tell that *here;* we all know well (with a sigh) for what you are *qualified*."

I had nothing to reply to such a compliment. The solemn Thing twinkled its eyes, rolled its head about like a china Mandarin, and, when it seemed firmly balanced on its shoulders, continued with a smile of ineffable self-complacency,—

"You are thinking who are the Editors?"

Really I was thinking no such thing; but he looked so well-pleased, I had not the heart to contradict him.

Metrical Legends to vol. i. in 1821, and one on Goethe's *Faust* to vol. ii. in 1822 (Mr. Anderson's "Bibliography" appended to Dr. Garnett's *Life of Thomas Carlyle*). See Norton, *Early Letters of Thomas Carlyle*, ii., pp. 53, 252. "The *New Edinburgh Review*, Waugh's, is with the spirits of its Fathers! They gave it up last number": he says, "so perish all Queen Common-sense's enemies!"

"And pray, Sir, who are they?"

"We do not wish ourselves to be known," said he; "but I may mention to *you* that Peter Dodds and I are to be principal Editors."

"And who is Peter Dodds?"

"Provost Dodds' son."

"Indeed! I thought I had been at school with all *his* family. I did not know he had a son of that name."

"Oh! Peter went to school *long after you left it*."

"What! You do not mean that the *boy* who is in Mr. Davidson's office is going to be Editor of a Magazine?"

"The same! He is a very clever *young man*."

"Mr. Cunningham," said I, with all the gravity I could muster, "Mr. Tait is a decent, industrious lad, and I am of opinion that the first step to be taken in this business is to secure him against being ruined."

"Oh! Peter Dodds and I mean to do that. There is no fear of Mr. Tait."

I next proceeded to exercise all my powers of

argument in trying to convince this candidate for literary fame, that it would be more advisable for the hitherto *latent* genius of Haddington to distribute itself among the various periodical works in the Metropolis, when, if not admired, the strength of others would sustain their *weakness*, and they might *hope to pass unobserved*, instead of, by uniting in a body, rendering *darkness visible.*

And the Creature, on his side, used every argument he was master of to induce me to take an active part in this most unpromising Magazine; which however I positively declined, at least till I was assured by the success of the first number that it would not go to the Devil.

We parted *mutually* amused (I believe) after an interview of more than an hour's length. And here ends my story. It may not seem *to you* so laughable as I led you to expect, for words cannot do it justice; but to me, who saw the Creature's pompous absurdity in all the vividness of reality, and who am moreover gifted with a somewhat *too* lively perception of the ridiculous—it was more than laughable—it was really *overpowering*. One night when it was very stormy, I lay awake till four o'clock in the morning, thinking on the perils of such a night at sea, and then the George and his Magazine came into my head, and the multitude of odd conceits my imagination suggested, operating on the nervousness occasioned by want of sleep, threw me into the most ungovernable fit of mirth I ever in my life experienced. The noise I made awoke my Mother, who, finding me lying at her side in a state of utter helplessness, sending forth loud and repeated "shouts of joy," fancied first I was dreaming, and then that I had gone mad; and she was really in a state of serious alarm before I could compose myself sufficiently to explain the occasion of my ill-timed transports. A tolerably well-expressed, printed plan of the work has been distributed among the inhabitants. I am sorry I have lost my copy. Mr. C. promised me a sight of the manuscript papers, from which I anticipate *great delight*. If the first number (which I dare swear will be the last) ever *gets out,* I will send it you.⁵

What dreadful weather this is! The very elements seem to have leagued with *that Wretch* against me; for it is impossible to hear such winds and not to *think* of him. God grant he may not be drowned! and that he may return to Scotland alive! Were he dead, you know I should forget his *faults;* and that—that would be dreadful. Could I ever forget *his faults?* He might then indeed have the *glory* of having made the proudest heart in Britain *break.* But do not—for mercy's sake do not *"pity"* me. I would almost as soon that people *should hate* as *pity* me. And shall I not be revenged? My revenge shall be great as his fault is great, and noble as his fault is base.

---

⁵ In spite of Miss Welsh's unfavourable opinion, it appears that Mr. George Tait "from 1822 to 1828 published and conducted *The East Lothian Magazine,* published monthly. It was supported by a number of the young *literati* of the locality, who contributed articles of ability in historical, agricultural, and general literature. It had a considerable circulation."—J. Martine, *Reminiscences of Haddington* (Edin., 1883), p. 12.

I forgot to mention *one* instance of his effrontery at our last meeting. Thinking that Janet Ewart might *remark* my *silence*, I summoned forth my fortitude, and enquired for Margaret. "She is very unwell," said he, "and wearying exceedingly to see you. *We* have been expecting you at 'Phantassie' for a long time. *I* wish you would go to-day. The carriage is up. I brought it for a Miss Wilson who has come from Edinburgh; so you had best just go with *us*." Oh the Devil incarnate! I have been once at Phantassie since he left it. It was *trying*, but I went through it *bravely*. Poor Margaret is now confined to bed—to all appearances dying. How could he leave her at such a time?—his favourite she was too. And yet perhaps it was to save his feelings from the melancholy—— But he has no feeling—none.

I have sacrificed a German lesson to you to-day, so I may perhaps be excused if I require a little of your time in return. Now, my dear, dear Angel Bessy (God help thee!), will you take the trouble to go to Brown's and pur-

chase for me a pair of very handsome crystal
jelly glasses⁶!!! as the comb is rather beyond
the dimensions of my purse, or rather of my
Mother's (for you know I never carry one). I
mean to ornament my *head* with THESE. (How
could you suppose I would be so extravagant
as to buy a coronet for myself?) My Mother
got beautiful jelly glasses from him for Mrs. W.
(who by the way has not written me *one word*
since she *got married*). Perhaps Mr. Brown
may remember them. And will you also, my
over-*adored* Bessy (*This* is further off), go to Gall
and Spurzheim⁷—no, Gall and Leckky, or some
such thing, and prevail on them to give you two
modest *little flowers* or a little wreath of white in
exchange for this *monster*. Janet Ewart heard
me complaining of having nothing to put on my
head at a party here one night, and when she re-

---

⁶ Can this be some kind of head-dress? Commentators differ.

⁷ The phrenologists. Spurzheim had been in Scotland "examining heads" not long before. See Norton, *Early Letters of Thomas Carlyle*, i., pp. 91, 94, 95, 136; ii., p. 252. "Leckky" is Jane Welsh's spelling: *qu.* Leckie?

turned to town very attentively sent me this; but it is far too *fashionable* for me—my head is quite lost in it. If you take one a little higher, they may perhaps be more willing to exchange it. And when all this is done, my *good* Bessy, send me the amount of my debt and Aggy's[?]. I would enclose money if I had it, but my mother's notes "be all done"! I send you some lines I got lately; give them to Mr. Aitken. They are more in *his way* than the *cheese*. Return him also my thanks for the *fun* he procured me. Ask David Ritchy,[8] if within reach of oracular communica-

---

[8] This, I suppose, is David Ritchie, afterwards minister of Tarbolton, Ayrshire. He was nephew and from 1826-29 assistant to Dr. William Ritchie, minister of the High Church and Professor of Divinity in the University of Edinburgh, on whom Carlyle has written a note in *Letters and Memorials of Jane Welsh Carlyle*, i., p. 196. He (David Ritchie) must at this time have been a student. He once told me that Jane Welsh lent him her tragedy to read, on condition that he gave "a written criticism." He could recollect nothing about it, except that it was "very wild and bloody," and that in the last act none of the *dramatis personæ* remained alive to speak the epilogue! (This must have been the tragedy written "before she was fourteen." "She used to speak of it 'as just an explosion,'" says Miss

tion, what Treatise on punctuation it was, which was recommended to him. Mr. Irving is making a horrible noise in London, where he has got a church. He tells me, in his last, that his head is quite turned with the admiration he has received; and really I believe him. The boys Mr. Carlyle is attending are Bullers (or some such name) with Dr. Fleming.⁹ They are *great Boys, singularly great*. But I will tell you all about my two learned friends in my next, for I am beginning to feel some remorse for having consumed such a quantity of vellum paper. Kiss Maggy and your Uncle for me! Give my compliments to Mr.

Jewsbury in *Reminiscences*, ed. Froude, ii., p. 79; ed. Norton, i., p. 60). He told me also—what is quite irrelevant, but is worth putting on record—that people thought it very wicked of Sam Aitken (often mentioned in these letters) to have a statuette of Napoleon in his room and to admire "the national enemy."

⁹ See Froude, *Thomas Carlyle*, A. i., p. 146; *Reminiscences*, ed. Froude, i., p. 193 ff.; ed. Norton, ii., p. 102 ff. This allusion and the reference to Irving (cf. Froude, *Thomas Carlyle*, A. i., p. 152 ff.) fix the date of this letter. The promise to tell "all about" Irving and Carlyle can hardly be said to be fulfilled in any of the following letters; but see pp. 65 and 78 in Letters IX. and XI.

McLeroth (I like him much better since I saw how his name is spelled), and tell him he is a person of *no enterprise*. Mr. Gordon is to preach to us on Wednesday, our fast-day. I have fished much for an invitation to dinner at the Doctor's, but I am beginning to despair. I dreamt of Dr. Chalmers all last night.

Yours very affectionately,
JANE WELSH.

You will be very ungrateful if you do not write me soon and long.

IX.

To Miss Stodart, 22 George Square, Edinburgh.

Favoured by Mr. McMim.[1]

TEMPLAND,

22nd July [1822 or 23?]

MY BELOVED COUSIN,—

I have one excuse to offer for my apparent forgetfulness of you, and of my promise. It is rather metaphysical in its nature, but there is "common sense" in it for all that.

---

[1] Mr. McMim must be the same person as the "Professor of Silence" referred to at the end of the letter (Mim = "mum.") One is tempted to suppose that this may be Carlyle. But Carlyle does not seem to have left Edinburgh at all in July of 1822 (see Norton, *Early Letters of Thomas Carlyle*, ii., pp. 93, 98), and he visited Dumfriesshire in October (Froude, *Thomas Carlyle*, A. i., p. 169). All through the summer of 1823 he appears to have been with the Bullers at Kinnaird House in Perthshire (Froude, *Thomas Carlyle*, A. i., p. 186). So that the tempting conjecture must be put aside. The reference to Irving would suit either year, but is rather more appropriate in the earlier. I cannot settle the date from the affairs of Benjamin B——.

However, as it would require at least two pages of my paper to explain it fully, and as I have other matters more interesting to discuss, I shall rely on your Christian charity in the meantime, confident of obtaining your full forgiveness when we meet.

If ever my excellent Mother gets me wheedled here again! Three weeks indeed! I conjectured how it would be from the very first. Oh my beloved German, my precious, precious time! Were there only some definite prospect of a release! but there is none. As long as our friends here press us to stay, my Mother will not stir; my only hope is in tiring them.

We have got my Uncle from Liverpool, his wife, the most horrid woman on the face of the earth, and five such children! in addition to our *family-party;* and what with the mother's scolding and the children's squalling, and my Uncle's fighting, and my Grandfather fidgetting, I am half-demented; and if some speedy alteration for the better does not take place in my condition, you may expect to hear of me being found drowned in the Nith or hanged in my garters.[2]

Now and then a visit to Penfillan or somewhere has afforded a little variety to my existence. The week before last I spent with my Uncle George at Boreland;[3] and such a week! There was no amusement within doors, and the weather precluded the possibility of finding any without. The only book in the house (*Cœlebs in Search of a Wife*) was monopolized by a young lady who, I strongly suspect, had come there upon Cœlebs's errand; and the rest of us had no sort of weapon whatever to combat time with. For four whole days I had nothing for it but to count the drops of rain that fell from the ceiling into a basin beneath; or to make a "*burble*"[4] of my watch-chain, for the satisfaction of undoing it. Oh Plato, Plato! what tasks!

---

[2] See *note* 3 to Letter XIII., p. 92.

[3] This is not a fictitious name.

[4] *Burble* = confusion, disorder (Fr. *barbouiller*). The word is used metaphorically by Carlyle in Letter XXXVII., p. 223.

At length in a phrensy of ennui I mounted a brute of a horse that could do nothing but trot, and rode thirty-two miles just for diversion. I left the good people at Boreland wondering, when it would be fair? they had wondered for four days, and when I came back they were still wondering. How few people retain their faculties in rainy weather!

I spent two days in Dumfries on my way back, and these two days were more interesting than the three hundred and sixty-five preceding ones. Who do you think was there at the selfsame time? My own gallant artist! Benjamin B—— himself! I fancied him still inhaling the atmosphere of Goethe, when I learned he was within a stone-cast of the spot I sat on! But I did not see him!!! or rather I did not speak with him; for I actually saw him—on the opposite bank of the river! Let any human being conceive a more tantalizing situation! saw him—and durst not make any effort to attract his notice, though, had my will alone been consulted in the matter, to have met him "*eyes to eyes* and *soul to soul*," I would have swam—ay, swam across, at the risk of being dosed with water-gruel for a month to come. Oh this everlasting etiquette! how many, and how ungrateful are the sacrifices it requires! Providence has surely some curious design respecting this youth and me! It was on my birthday[5] we parted a year ago; it was on my birthday we met or (but for that confounded river) should have met again. And there are many strange coincidences in our histories besides. Something *must* come out of all this! And yet it was strange in Providence, after bringing us together from such a distance, to leave us on the opposite banks of a river! I declare I do not know what to make of it; but time, time unravels all mysteries. And now whither is he gone? to the north, or to the south? I learned that his father had taken a seat in the English mail; but was it for himself or for his son?

---

[5] July 14 ("Bastille day").

I wonder what the devil keeps my Mother here?

We are off again to-morrow on another visit —to the Crichtons⁶ at Dabton. Mrs. C. is one of my first favourites. I hear William Gordon is to be married to a cousin of his own in Dumfries. I declare I cannot hear of these marryings and givings in marriage, without some feeling of irritation; but *espérance!* it is my motto.

What think you of the "*Great* centre of attraction," "*the Spanish Adonis*," "the renowned Edward Irving?"⁷ Did I not tell you how it would be? Oh! I *do* share in his triumph! but I fear—

---

⁶ The Crichtons of Dabton (she spells it "Chrighton" here) are mentioned in *Letters and Memorials of Jane Welsh Carlyle*, i., p. 74.

⁷ Cf. Froude, *Thomas Carlyle*, A. i., p. 152 ff. "Spanish Adonis" must refer to Irving's appearance. Here is Carlyle's description of him, as he first saw him in 1808: "Looked very neat, self-possessed, and enviable: a flourishing slip of a youth, with coal-black hair, swarthy clear complexion; very straight on his feet; and, except for the glaring squint alone, decidedly handsome."—*Reminiscences*, ed. Froude, i., p. 88; ed. Norton, ii., p. 17.

I greatly fear he has not a head for these London flatteries!

This travels by the "Proffessor (one f) of silence," as also Mr. Aitken's books and two pairs of shoes. The shoes I will thank you to get transmitted to Anderson; and I will likewise thank you remember me to Mr. Aitken, and to apologise to him for my having detained these books so long. I never liked risking them by the coach, and this is the first opportunity that has occurred. The parcel will be left at the shop.

Everybody here except *the woman*—who knows nothing at all about you—unites with me in kind love to yourself and Brady. Remember me, according to your discretion, to all my acquaintances you know.

Write to me, if you *can* forgive me, and believe me

Always affectionately yours,
JANE B. WELSH.

X.

[This letter must belong to the latter part of January, 1823. King George IV. visited Edinburgh in the latter part of August, 1822.]

To Miss Stodart, 22 George Square, Edinburgh.

Honor'd by Mr. John W——.

HADDINGTON,

Tuesday.

IT is over! my dearest cousin! Heaven be praised, the "*grand veesit*" is over! They—to wit, that pattern of a wise man, my Uncle Robert, his big, bouncing brute of a dog, and pretty, *proper*, prosaic wife—took themselves off last Saturday morning. Since Miss Betty Grey, of curious memory, stept into "*The Good Intent*,"[1] summer was a year, I think I have not

---

[1] A Haddington correspondent informs me that "The Good Intent" was the name of a coach which ran between Haddington and Edinburgh. "It took about three hours and more sometimes to perform the journey with the same pair of horses."—J. Martine, *Reminiscences of Haddington*, p. 18.

sent so hearty a "get ye good morning, Audrey" after any departing visitor.

After keeping two honest Linton hens in an indescribable state of anxiety for a whole fortnight, and precluding *us* from enjoying any Christmas civilities our neighbours might proffer us, they came just on the day we did not expect them, for it rained *atrociously*, and just on the day we did not want them, for my Mother and I were particularly engaged. She—that is our Mother—was making nice things, and ourself was in the act of toasting a clean, cold handkerchief before the fire—in preparation for the last scene of Schiller's *Wallenstein*,[3] the most tragical of tragedies—when the door burst open, and the young person who has the honour to be our Aunt-in-Law, sailed in in all the pride of

---

[2] Seems to be a vague reminiscence of *As You Like It*, Act v., Sc. i. where Audrey says, "God ye good even, William."

[3] Spelt with one *l*. She had cried over *Wallenstein* some weeks before this. "You did well to cry so heartily over *Wallenstein*," writes Carlyle to her on Dec. 25th, 1822 (Norton, *Early Letters of Thomas Carlyle*, ii., p. 156).

furs and feathers, followed by her Husband, in a shooting dress, and preceeded by the inimitable Dargo—that Dog of Dogs, "*la huitième merveille du monde*"—prancing, capering, and overthrowing, with all the boldness and impudence to be expected in a town dog on a visit to *friends in the country*. However, to do Dargo justice, he seems the most kindly disposed of the three; for he no sooner descried Shandy, than he made straight up to him, and commenced kissing and caressing him with great good-will. Shandy, unacquainted with town manners, approved not of such freedom, nor was he slow in showing his resentment, for that brief morsel, like the offspring of the bass-fiddle,[4] has a bigger soul than his size entitled him to: his eyes lightened, his back bristled, like a very cat's, and he poured forth such a volley of indignation, that the canine Goliath, quite astounded by his eloquence, made a rapid retreat with his tail between his legs. This hub-bub deserves the notice I have taken of

---

[4] The little fiddle being the child of the big fiddle.

it; for it was the only moment of excitement I experienced during their stay.

Oh! I have been enduring the pains of purgatory for the last fortnight.[5] The sweet people hereabouts, fiddling, feasting, and capering away their wits, as if they had heard a blast from Oberon's horn—all for joy that they have got one step nearer to the close of their pitiful existence—were of themselves sufficient to have thrown me into a wonderful state of quandary; and then within doors! "*O Gemini and gilliflower water!*" could you have had a peep within! There was my precious Uncle, sneezing, snarling, and sometimes snoring; *the Lady* dressing, yawning, and practising postures; our Mother wearying her heart to entertain them—all in vain; and our sorrowful self casting many a wistful glance towards the little table, where our good friends Schiller and Alfieri lay neglected, and wishing from time to time our cold visitors in hotter quarters than they might have found to their liking.

---

[5] The "new year" time.

You may think me bitter—perhaps inconstant towards these gentry—may be so! I certainly once loved Robert truly—for no reason I can discover, but his being my uncle. I looked to him as a protector and a friend when I needed both; and I have found him as indifferent to my interests as any stranger. The warm affection I offered him deserved something better than bare toleration, and even *that* it hath scarcely found. "*Slighted love is ill to bear,*"[6] as the song says, and I am no miracle of patience. I have knocked at the door of his "*hard and stony heart*" till my knuckles are sore; it hath not *been opened unto me*, and of a verity I will knock no longer. As for the Lady, with her cold routine of looks and words, her affectation and insipidities, she delights not me; "*my soul is above her.*" Moreover she once called a certain witty, dashing, accomplished friend of mine "*a heavy-looking* LAD." Oh, the indiscriminating ass! I will

---

[6] "Slighted love is sair to bide," occurs in Burns's *Duncan Gray.*

never forgive her for it! never! But what
could be expected from Port Glasgow? She
may look on the physiognomy of muslins, and
understand, but of "the *luminous characters of
the soul, impressed upon the brow*," her obtuse
mind hath no conception! Away with them!
it is an unworthy subject.

David S—— is to be speedily married to
Miss R——'s thousand pounds. *Espérance, ma
chère!* When such women as Miss R—— get
Lieutenants, *we* shall have generalissimos at
least. Thomas Gillespie is to be here next
week. Captain Spalding[7] is waiting till next
month *for a friend*, whom Miss Mair says I
know well; but I do *not* know well, nor can I

---

[7] "Captain Spalding" is mentioned in a letter of Carlyle
to Miss Welsh (Jan. 20th, 1823), given in Norton's *Early
Letters of Thomas Carlyle*, ii., p. 178. "I am sorry for
you with your Highland cousin and the gallant Captain
Spalding. But it is wrong in you to take these things
so much to heart. A little interruption does no harm
at all, and these visits, as they bring you more in contact
with the common world, are in your case absolutely beneficial." She had evidently complained of their visitors to
Carlyle, as she does at the beginning of this letter.

imagine who she alludes to. If it is somebody coming to woo, I will send him to you, for I mean to be a *belle* for these eighteen months to come. What a bright creature Hope is, after all! But to the point. I suppose our visit to town must remain *in prospectu* for some weeks longer, till these good people are come and gone. Well, time flies swift enough; it is already six months to-day since the day before we went to Edinburgh to see the King.[8] I expect to *like* Edinburgh next time, which I have not done in my late visits there. For God's sake, Bess, never let there be any more coolnesses betwixt

---

[8] George IV. landed on Aug. 15th, 1822, and left Edinburgh on Aug. 29th. Carlyle's reflections on the royal visit will be found in *Reminiscences*, ed. Froude, i., p. 173; ed. Norton, ii., p. 85. "Reading, one day, on a public Placard from the Magistrates (of which there had been several), That on His Majesty's Advent it was to be expected that everybody would be carefully well dressed, 'black coat and white duck trousers,' if at all convenient,—I grumbled to myself 'Scandalous flunkeys, I, if I were changing my dress at all, should incline rather to be in white coat and black trousers!'—but resolved rather to quit the City altogether, and be absent and silent in such efflorescence of flunkeyisms."

us; they go to my heart, tho' I can look proud enough all the time. Give Jane Welsh's respectful compliments to Mr. Aitken, and request of him to display his best taste in the beautifying of my wee, wee Cicero. The *pigmæi* race are likely to be in fashion this season, and I am desirous to have the little elf superbly dressed. Have you seen the Simpson lately? Do you know he has been guilty of plagiarism, or, at best, of most servile imitation, in one of those poems of his. You remember "as the core-blasted tree," etc., etc.? It is the best thing he ever wrote. Well, in looking over some scraps of verse the other day, I found a beautiful passage from Moore's *Melodies*, that has indubitably been the mother of "the core-blasted tree." How provoking!

"As a beam o'er the face of the waters may glow,
 While the tide runs in coldness and darkness below;
 So the cheek may be tinged with a warm sunny smile,
 While the cold heart to ruin runs darkly the while." [9]

---

[9] The first stanza of a song in Moore's *Irish Melodies*, the first line serving as title. In the second line Moore wrote "in darkness and coldness."

Pray ask him which he thinks has expressed the sentiment best, he or Moore? Adieu, my darling! my play time is done, or I would not take leave of you yet, for I am in a scribbling humor to-day. My piano has been tuned, and "The Blue Bell" sounds divinely. Ta-ta; kisses to Brady and Maggie.

Your affectionate
JANE B. WELSH.

What a pity but Mr. Micklew (oh! I have forgot to spell it again) roth[10] (I think) had a right look of me! He seems to be labouring under a strange mistake.

---

[10] Cf. p. 59

XI.

To Miss Stodart, 22 George Square, Edinburgh.

HADDINGTON,

Sunday [Postmark, *March* 31*st*, 1823].

MY DEAREST COUSIN,—

I have commenced two letters for you during the last two weeks, and each time I have been interrupted by that Ass of Asses, John W——. To-day I am safe till the church comes out. Was there ever anything more provoking? We are to have no war after all; our travellers on the continent will be exposed to no inconveniences; and so—well! no matter! it is better to keep company with Schiller and De Staël for one half year, than to "*suckle fools and chronicle beer*"[1] for half a century.

I am going to forget him immediately. I could have done so long ago, but for one little action,

---

[1] "To suckle fools and chronicle small beer."—*Othello*, Act ii., Sc. i. Is George Rennie the "traveller on the continent"?

that has made a strange impression on my senses. My spur required to be shifted from my left foot to my right; and you cannot think with what inimitable grace this small manœuvre was accomplished. Whenever his idea occurs to me, I fancy him with one knee on the earth, his horse's bridle flung across his arm, his hands employed in fastening the spur, and his eloquent eyes fixed assuredly *not* on what he was doing. Dear Bess, is it not very extraordinary that a philosopher, as I am or pretend to be, should be so taken with an attitude? However I *will* forget him. Hitherto I have been twice as constant as Penelope; *she* was encouraged by the assurance that, as soon as Ulysses *came*, her troubles were at an end: but *I* have no such comfortable certainty.

Really there is nothing at all amusing in one's mode of existence here. A tea-party, a quarrel, or a *report* of a marriage now and then, are the only excitements this precious little borough affords. However I battle away with Time pretty successfully; my lessons employ the greater part of the day, and a little trifling with the "*professional callers,*" or a game at chess or battledoor with our *constant* man of physic, Dr. Fyffe, consumes the rest. Often at the end of the week my spirits and my industry begin to flag; but then comes one of Mr. Carlyle's brilliant letters, that inspires me with new resolution, and brightens all my hopes and prospects with the golden hues of his own imagination. He is a very Phœnix of a Friend! Sometimes too Providence prepares me a little extra entertainment. For instance, about a month ago, in one of the dirtiest, darkest lanes in a most untidy part of the town, I found—you could never guess what! I actually found *a Genius!* The said Genius is a beggar-boy about fifteen years of age; he lives with his mother (an ugly old sinner) in a sort of cell about four feet square. Never had Genius a more unpromising abode! A palsied table, a one-legged stool, the wreck of a bed, and a sort of wooden press are all the articles of furniture it contains. But in spite of its abject poverty the place has a look of comfort, I may almost say of *taste.* Its black mud walls are plastered over with heads, maps, landscapes, and caricatures; a neat little model of a man-of-war is mounted on brackets above the chimney; and the table is oppressed with books so smoked and so tattered they might to all appearance date their antiquity from Noah's Ark. All the drawings and the man-of-war are the boy's own work; and the most of his time, in spite of the obstacles of poverty and ignorance, is devoted to the cultivation of taste far superior to his state and education.

My ideas of talent are so associated with everything great and noble, that while I admired the boy's ardour and ambition, it never once occurred to me a Genius might possibly be a knave; and so I spent my leisure time for one whole fortnight in laying plans for his improvement in the arts, and anticipating the splendid career of successful enterprise that lay before him. But about the end of that time I began to suspect my subject might disappoint my lofty expectations. He discovered a mortal aversion to all kinds of vulgar labour—that was genius-like; he had never undergone the operation of baptism

—that was quite romantic: but there were other points of his character and history which I could not so easily away with. He is greedy, cunning, and ungrateful; this disgusted me, and when I found no power on earth could prevail with him to refrain from lying or to wash his face, I lost all patience. My plans had given him so much *éclat* that my patronage was no longer necessary, and so I left the *patient* in the hands of his new admirers. The genius was succeeded in my affection by an Irish packman with a broken back—eight years old and a few inches high— a calm, correct, decided character, the very reverse of the artist. He hops about with a crutch under one arm and a basket on the other; and with his profits on tape and chapel needles[2] helps to maintain three sisters younger than himself.

---

[2] "Chapel needles," *i.e.* Whitechapel needles. I have before me the label of a packet of needles, kindly sent by a correspondent from Alyth, on which "White Chapel" is printed as two separate words. Another correspondent tells me that her mother, now over ninety, remembers an old woman who " liked a darning needle to sew everything with." She used to say, "Awa' wi' your whites and chapels!

But my paper is getting filled, and I have not given you one word of news. Poor Jane Lorimer, Margaret's only sister, is just dying of fever; she has been past hope for the last week. Miss R——[3] is to be married on *the first of April.* The unfortunate couple have shown the little sense they have in selecting *that* day. Poor girl! she is apparently in a galloping consumption, and it will be a miracle if ever she set her foot on Indian ground; but if her purse is safe, David will not vex himself about her lungs. I had a letter from Mrs. Keith the other day; she is quite in the second heaven. I wonder you have not heard of Dr. Keith. He is brother to the Knight Marischal,[4] and has a library as famous as the

---

Commend me to the derner." Another tells me of a pedlar-woman who went about the Lothians, and used to say : " Ye may brag as ye like o' your chapels and your sharps. Commend me to the darner for our Jock's sarks [*i.e.* shirts]." For the fame of Whitechapel needles, compare Dickens's *Christmas Carol:* " For the sharpest needle, best Whitechapel, warranted not to cut in the eye, was not sharper than Scrooge."

[3] See preceding letter, p. 72.

[4] Alexander Keith, Knight-Marischal of Scotland, is men-

Marischal's little pony. He is very clever and frightfully plain; but then he has a carriage and a fine footman, and what defects do not these supply? My Mother has said nothing of *the day*, though we are always speaking of the grand visit. I am so out of humour about it, that I am resolved I shall not ask again; but I fervently hope she will tell you *when* before long. Kind love and kisses to Bradie and Maggie. I fear you will not be able to decipher this fearful scrawl. Do you know? I have got a fine head of hair lately; altogether I am looking rather more captivating than usual. I pray Venus it may last till I get to town.

Yours affectionately for ever and ever,
JANE BAILLIE WELSH.

There is some chance of George Rennie paying a visit to Phantassie during the spring or summer. I was surprised to hear it, but I do not believe he will come.

---

tioned in Lockhart's *Life of Scott* in connexion with the visit of George IV.

XII.

To Miss Bess Stodart of the Easton,[1] *etc., etc., etc.*

HADDINGTON,

18*th April* [1824?].

MY SWEETEST COZ,—

I have been meaning to write to thee for these last three weeks—but "man proposeth and God disposeth!" I do not know how it is, for all such a miser as I am as to the article of time, I have very seldom an hour to spare. I am busy just now translating German—as busy as if my fortune in this world, and my salvation in that which is to come, depended on my proficiency in that enchanting tongue; and then there has been Miss Grace[2] here for a whole month, and she needs the entertainment of walks and tea-parties. At the first she was quite intoler-

---

[1] A farm near Biggar, in Lanarkshire, where Eliza Stodart was born.

[2] Her aunt.

able with her fine-lady airs, and "*toploftical*"³ notions. She thought (I suppose) that she was to carry it over me with as high a hand *here* as she had done at Penfillan; but I was not just in the humour to let her. "*My foot is on my native heath, and my name is McGregor!*"⁴ There no one shall play *the* Miss Welsh but *me*. She decamps to-morrow—Praise be to God in the highest! for I am "*sick of imitating Job*" for this bout. We have had Miss Macmillan too for ten days, and her brother for two, both of them right worthy persons in their way, whom one does not grudge to "*behave pretty*" to.

Speaking of pretty behaviour, you may tell Mr. Tiger⁵ that I should think *he* has behaved very ugly indeed. What was the use of making such a hubbub about my friend's address unless he meant to call for him? Moray Street is

---

³ *Top-loft* = top storey, highest gallery; so *toploftical* = high and mighty.

⁴ *Rob Roy*, chap. xxxiv.

⁵ Perhaps this is her cousin "Teeger Wull," Tiger Will —William Dunlop, referred to in *Letters and Memorials*, ii., p. 335.

neither a habitation in the moon nor in the centre of the earth. As far as my geography helps me, it is a new street half way down Leith Walk; but it is no matter now where it is! *Mr. Thomas* has been in the country this month back, and the information he wished to obtain from Mr. Gillies by means of the Tiger's introduction he has long ago gotten from another quarter.[6]

I have had a horrible fright with Mother. She was taken last Monday with a violent pain in

---

[6] Carlyle writes from 3 Moray Street on April 2nd, 1824; he writes from Mainhill on April 15th (Froude, *Thomas Carlyle*, A. i., pp. 210, 212). Likely enough she may exaggerate the time he has been out of town. The reference to Mr. Gillies points to 1824 as the date of this letter; for Carlyle writes to his brother Alexander on March 2nd, 1824, from 1 Moray Street: "There is one Pearse Gillies, an advocate here, who knows of me, and whom I am to see on the subject of this book [*Wilhelm Meister*]; he being a great German scholar, and having a fine library of books, one or two of which I wish to examine" (Norton, *Early Letters of T. Carlyle*, ii., p. 267). "Mr. Robert Pearse Gillies," says Prof. Norton, "was a man of much culture, who had resided in Germany, and seen Goethe and other celebrities. He had a large acquaintance with literary people in England and Scotland, and his *Memoirs of a Literary Veteran*, published in three volumes in 1851, contains many entertaining sketches and anecdotes." Moray Street is now Spey Street.

her head and retching. Mr. Howden[7] bled her, employed all sorts of vigorous remedies; but in spite of everything that was done she remained for more than three hours in a state of agony that I never saw the like of. Since then she has had no return of violent illness, but she is still plagued with headache and sickness at times. However, as it is visibly bile that is at the bottom of all the mischief, I expect with the help of a few *abominations* to have her quite put to rights in a day or two.

I need not say how happy we were to hear of your Uncle's amendment. Is it not very odd that, sensible man as he is, he cannot take care of himself? You never quit him that he is not laid up. As a little Dunlop said of her Father once when he had put them all in a panic by staying out, "*If ony body wud ha[u]d his hands, I would cuff his lugs*[8] *to him.*" In the meantime you may give him a kiss.

---

[7] Mr. Thomas Howden, surgeon, who had been Dr. Welsh's partner, afterwards lived in her old Haddington home (*Letters and Memorials*, ii., p. 321).   [8] *I.e.* box his ears.

I have run against the little gunpowder man of medicine,[9] in the entry, several times. We "mowe"[10] to one another. I toss my head 'toploftically'; he looks as if he could eat me; and that is all. A week or two after we came from Edinburgh he tried another fit of illness; but it did nothing for him, and as we neither sent to enquire for him, nor testified sympathy for him in any way, *his sins were very soon forgiven him;*[11] that is to say, after having kept his bed for a week, one day dabbling with leeches, and the next plashing in warm water, he all at once rose up in goodhealth, dressed himself, and drove to town to be present at an operation performed on his uncle, not the musical genius of St. Giles' Steeple, but a fat old gentleman who has a fine house with a "*Hall*" and *saloons* and *grounds* about it in the vicinity of Moffat. Now, when

---

[9] Dr. Fyffe. See Letter V., p. 25.

[10] *Mow* = " to make mouths "—smile or grin, as the case may be.

[11] " For whether is easier, to say, Thy sins be forgiven thee; or to say, Arise, and walk ? " (Matt. ix. 5.)

he perceives that he may bleed or boil himself to the day of Pentecost without interesting this *hard and stony heart* of mine in the least in his favour, he is adopting another mode of attack. Instead of *shaving his whiskers* and using all possible expedients to give him the aspect of a woebegone man, he is now trying to dazzle my wits with a white hat, silver-headed jockey whip, and bits of *leggings* of so bright a yellow that it does me ill to look at them: but *c'est assez!*

George Rennie is to be home on a visit in the beginning of June; that is nothing either to you or me.

Now, my *dear, dear angel Bessie*, will you do me two tremendous favours? Will you send the book in the first place to *Doctor* Carlyle's[12] lodgings, where Betty[13] was before, as I have forgot the name of the people? I dare not commit it to the *indiscretion* of a porter. Next, you are to

---

[12] Thomas Carlyle's brother John, then a student of medicine in Edinburgh.

[13] Probably the old Haddington nurse. See *note* 10 to Letter V., p. 27.

be so very kind as order for me at Gibson[14] and Craig's one of the best gentleman's hats, of the most fashionable cut, *not* broadrimmed. The *outside* measure is inclosed. It is to be a present to my intended husband; so do see that they send a *Jemmy*[15] one. I am in haste, as this insipid scrawl bears ample witness. Mother joins in kind, kind love to Bradie and you.

Ever, dearly beloved, your affectionate friend,
JANE B. WELSH.

Mr. Howden has not called to-night, so I cannot get at the measure of his head; but I will send it by the first opportunity.[16]

---

[14] She spells it with two b's. Above, "abomination" had two m's—perhaps through a sort of emphasis, as I have known a soldier write to his mother from India, "It is very hottt here."

[15] *I.e.* spruce, dandyish.

[16] This *P.S.* is written outside, and she has afterwards drawn her pen through it. If "my intended husband" means Carlyle, she must have taken Eliza Stodart into her confidence (as seems to be implied in Letter XI., p. 77). But then one must conjecture that Carlyle's head was of the same size as Mr. Howden's, which appears to be doubtful. If the odd present of "a *jemmy* hat" had been a joke, "intended husband" would have been underlined.

XIII.

To Miss Stodart, 22 George Square, Edinburgh.

Templand,

27th September [Postmark, 1824].

My dearest Eliza,—

I promised to write to you as soon as I was settled. "Lord! how this world is given to lying!"[1] I have been settled now near a month, and you are still without your letter. *Eh bien!* fortunately for me, you are too good to get *crumpy*.[2]

The Fates have been indifferently kind to me since we parted. During the two weeks my Cousin stayed with us I never wearied once. I played chess or écarté with him; paid morning

---

[1] *Falstaff.* "Lord, Lord, how this world is given to lying!" (*First Part of King Henry IV.*, Act v., Sc. 4.)

[2] *Crumpie* is explained by Jamieson "crisp," "brittle": so, figuratively, it would mean "irritable." But probably the meaning is influenced by *grumpy*.

visits with him; strolled thro' the woods and fields with him, or sat on a green bank and talked sentiment with him. You will stare to hear of Mr. Baillie talking sentiment: I assure you nevertheless, this man with moustaches and four rings on his fingers is as sentimental as the Prince of Denmark. But it is only in confidential intercourse that he lays aside his dress-manner of indifference, and suffers all the sensibility of his heart to appear: even then he seems to take pleasure in gainsaying his nature. Often in our conversations, when his imagination had risen to the highest pitch, when his fine eyes full of tears, and the melancholy, impassioned tones of his voice showed he was ready to be overpowered by his feelings, he would start away to some theme of ridicule or folly, and efface the impression he had just made with the laugh of a Mephistopheles. How ill I understood him before we came here! His character has received such a fictitious colouring from the associations to which it has been exposed, that it might well deceive so unpractised an observer as I am!

"You were sure that he was not a person at all to *my* taste." *Lord help your simplicity!* how you mistook the matter! He is my very *beau-idéal* in all respects but one. His nature is the most affectionate I ever knew, his spirit the most magnificent; he has a clear, quick intellect, a lively fancy: with beauty, brilliance, sensibility, native gracefulness, and courtly polish, he wants but *genius* to be—the destiny of my life. What a pity that Heaven should have denied him this *sine qua non!* or rather what a mercy! for he will soon be married (I suppose) to that vexatious "somebody," and I have not, like my "unfortunate" namesake in the song, any fancy for dangling in my garters.[3] Well!

---

[3] This is an allusion to the ballad of *The Unfortunate Miss Bailey*, popular about 1805, and said to have first appeared in George Colman's *Love Laughs at Locksmiths*. It is to be found in Ingledew's *Ballads and Songs of Yorkshire* (1860), p. 241. The first stanza is as follows:

"A captain bold of Halifax, who dwelt in country quarters,
Seduced a maid, who hanged herself one morning in her garters.
His wicked conscience smited him, he lost his stomach daily,
He took to drinking ratafia, and thought upon Miss Bailey.
    Oh, Miss Bailey! Unfortunate Miss Bailey!"

[For this note I am indebted to my friend Mr. C. H. Firth.]

I begin to think men and women may be very charming, without having any *genius*. Who knows but I shall grow reasonable at last, descend from my ideal heaven to the real earth, marry, and—Oh Plato!—make a pudding? I do not say puddings; for sure I am, the first would be the death of me.

Eh bien! happen what may, I do not think I shall ever be Mrs. Benjamin B——. Oh, Jupiter! that broad-brimmed hat and calico great-coat! I shall never forget how he looked, so different from the long-cherished picture of him in my

---

Jane Welsh was called "Baillie" after her mother's mother, "a good and beautiful Miss Baillie," " of somewhat noted kindred in Biggar country" (*Reminiscences*, ed. Froude, ii., pp. 117, 128; ed. Norton, i., pp. 134, 154). "My Jeanie was called 'Jane Baillie Welsh' at the time of our marriage; but after a good few years, when she took to signing, 'Jane *Welsh* Carlyle,' in which I never hindered her, [why should he?] dropped the 'Baillie,' I suppose as too long. I have heard her quiz about 'the unfortunate Miss Baillie' of the song at a still earlier time " (*ib.*, ed. Froude, ii., p. 128; ed. Norton, i., pp. 154, 155). Did she not perhaps drop the name "Baillie," because of associations connected with it, or, rather, because afterwards it interested her no more? It is underlined in the signature to this letter.

mind! And so the meeting I so much desired has dispelled the illusion of more than two years! Do you know? the vulgar cast of his countenance, and the volley of nonsense he overwhelmed me with gave a shock to my nervous system, which it did not recover for four and twenty hours. Indeed to this day I turn sick at heart when I think of him. *Mais n'importe!* it is only one more Spanish castle[1] demolished; another may start up like a mushroom in its place!

I long for the last week of October, tho' I like the country better this season than I ever did before. Our *popularity* here is not a whit diminished; which is rather to be wondered at, as we are no novelty now. Ever since Mr. Baillie went away we have been "*on the transit from one friend's house to another*"; and as our acquaintances here are, for the most part, pleasant people, and see a deal of good company, I have no doubt that, could I be happy in idleness, I should find my present mode of life

---

[1] *Château en Espagne.*

agreeable enough. But the thought that "*life is short and art is long*"⁵ will not leave me at rest in idleness; it flashes upon my mind in the midst of amusement, and turns "*earth's vain, fading, vulgar show*" to weariness and vexation of spirit. The Menteith family have been wonderfully *affectionate* to me since I came here. The eldest son and daughter are amiable, intelligent, and particularly pleasing in their manners. Miss Menteith reads German, and is almost as fond of it as I am. The rest I hardly like. We have likewise received great attention from another family, whom we did not visit last season —the Gordons at Eccles. Captain Gordon is a well-looked,⁶ kind-hearted, gentlemanly man; his Lady is unlovely, but clever and well informed. She would be uncommonly agreeable, if she had not the misfortune to be born a Duke's

---

⁵ The familiar *Ars longa, vita brevis* comes originally from Hippocrates, Ὁ βίος βραχὺς, ἡ δὲ τέχνη μακρή—where the "art" is properly the art of medicine. The next quotation I cannot recognise.

⁶ *I.e.* well-favoured (cf. "well-spoken").

niece. I heard of Burns[7] being in our neighbourhood the other day, and entertaining a party with the private history of the Baillies. I wish to Heaven he had had a banknote plaster on his mouth![8] I have gone nowhere since without being assailed with "Is so and so the case? I was told it by a *man from Edinburgh.*" A pretty like man from Edinburgh to be sure! Will you remember me to Sam Aitken, and bid him send my little books by one of the coaches? I will return those he lent me as soon as I can possibly get done with them. There was a letter from Dugald the other day, full of inanities. I think he appears to be *out* of love. Kiss your Uncle for me. All here join in kindest regards to you and him. Write soon, and believe me always your attached friend

JANE *BAILLIE* WELSH.

---

[7] Probably *not* Gilbert Burns, the poet's brother, whom Carlyle saw on his first visit to Haddington (Norton, *Early Letters of Thomas Carlyle*, i., p. 353; cf. ii., p. 327; *Letters* [Second Series], i., p. 57), but an Edinburgh "writer."

[8] *Query*, "a *douceur* to make him keep his mouth shut"? or is the wish to be taken more literally?

P.S.—Miss B—— is in Glasgow! she wrote to me from Versailles about six weeks ago, assuring me that she would never visit Scotland again. "*How d——d odd!*"⁹ I am tired out with her *imprudence* and instability. Has Maggy¹⁰ got a pair of boys yet?

---

⁹ Seems to have been a pet phrase of James Baillie (see Letter XIV., pp. 103, 104; and XVI., p. 114); and he pervades this letter.

¹⁰ Margaret Stodart, Eliza's sister, was married on July 28th, 1824, to John Dudgeon (cf. Letter XVI., p. 115, and Letter XX., p. 131). She is generally referred to, after this, as "Mrs. John."

XIV.

To Miss Stodart, 22 George Square.

HADDINGTON,

18*th January* [1825?].

AMIABLE COUSIN,—

I said to myself, weeks ago, that I would write to you with the books. Now then the books are finished, and here I am writing. I might perhaps have been tempted to anticipate my purpose, if I had had anything worth while to communicate; but my history, since we parted, has been uninteresting to the last degree; and it would only have been *ennuying* you to send you any fragments of it.

From this you may conclude that I have been rather happy as otherwise. I have had no cause of rejoicing, neither have I had any of complaint. My little universe has been at rest from all sorts of commotion; has been "*calm and unruffled as a summer's sea when not a breath of wind flies o'er its surface* ";[1] or as a summer's quagmire (to use a more appropriate simile). The only event which has jarred the music of my soul for any length of time was a visit from Dugald G——, a most impudent and improper visit, "*all the circumstances of the case considered*"[2] (as Mr. A—— would say). He came uninvited, and stayed a week, stomaching the most *du haut en bas* treatment from me all the while. One would have thought that even the patience of an Indian must have rebelled under it; but *this* Dugald *creatur*[3] belongs to the spaniel genus (I opine); the more he is kicked about, the more he fawns and cringes. I told him, among other things, in tolerably plain English, that he was given to lying! (and good reason I had for saying so.) In reply, he kissed my hand! *This* was obeying the Scriptures with a vengeance. If I had bid

---

[1] "Calm and unruffled as a summer sea,
When not a breath of wind flies o'er its surface."
  Addison, *Cato*, Act i., Sc. 4.
[2] Cf. Letter V., p. 22.
[3] Allusion to *Rob Roy*, chap. xxii.

him get out at the door, I suppose he would have taken me in his arms. Drivelling, meanspirited, "thrice doubled ass"! He is sunk immeasurable fathoms deep in my disdain! "*Mais doucement*, Mademoiselle! there is no use of putting yourself in a passion. The young gentleman *is* a mooncalf, *that* nobody will deny you; but he is at present sixteen miles off, and not likely to disturb your equanimity again"—*c'est bien!*

On the other hand, the most pleasurable thing which has befallen me was receiving *two* packets from England in the same night: the one, a letter of *fifteen pages* from Mr. Baillie; the other a collection of autographs from his Opposite. What do you think? among these were a letter from Goethe,[4] and a fragment of a letter from

---

[4] Writing to Miss Welsh from London on December 20th, 1824, Carlyle says of this letter of Goethe: "I will copy it, for it is in a character you cannot read; and send it to you with the original, which you are to keep as the most precious of your literary relics. Only the last line and the signature are in Goethe's hand: I understand he *constantly* employs an amanuensis. Do you transcribe my copy and your own translation of it into the blank leaf of that German paper,

Byron! *Goethe's* was written to Mr. Carlyle himself. It is highly complimentary; and coming from the man whom he honours, almost to idolatry, must have gratified him beyond measure. I question if a charter of nobility could have gratified him as much. The other was given him by Procter (Barry Cornwall).[5] You cannot think how it affected me! This, then, was *his* handwriting! *his* whose image had haunted my imagination for years and years; whose wild, glorious spirit had tinctured all the poetry of my being! *he*, then, had seen and touched this very paper. I could almost fancy that his look and touch were visible on it! And *he*—where was he now? All the sentiment in me was screwed up to the highest pitch; I could

---

before you lay it by; that the same sheet may contain some traces of him whom I most venerate and her whom I most love in this strangest of all possible worlds."—Norton, *Early Letters of Thomas Carlyle*, ii., p. 292; cf. Froude, *Thomas Carlyle*, A. i., p. 265.

[5] She spells them "Proctor," "Cornwal." For Carlyle's acquaintance with Procter, cf. Froude, *Thomas Carlyle*, A. i., p. 220; Norton, *Early Letters*, ii., p. 289; *Reminiscences*, ed. Froude, i., p. 233; ed. Norton, ii., pp. 133, 134.

hardly help crying like a child or Dugald G——, and I kissed the seal with a fervour which would have graced the most passionate lover.[6]

---

[6] Cf. Letter VI., p. 30, where the greatest of tempters would take the shape of Lord Byron. For her feelings on hearing of Byron's death (1824) see Froude, *Thomas Carlyle*, A. i., p. 214. Along with these letters I found some verses on Byron in Jane Welsh's writing, dated "1816." The date was originally written 1817, and then corrected to 1816. In 1816 she was fifteen years old. They are as follows :

>Still, my loved Minstrel, I admire
>The strains of thy enchanted lyre :
>Still thy sad lays, so wildly sweet,
>I read, and while I read I weep.
>Nor do I check the burning tear,
>For 'tis a silent tribute, dear
>To souls like thine, which would inspire
>Each breast with sympathetic fire.
>Byron, thy noble, lofty mind
>Has been the sport of passions blind ;
>Phrenzy has havocked in thy brain,
>With all her desolating train.
>But that is past—and now you roam
>Far from your wife, your child, your home,
>Joys which might still have been your own.
>But shall I love my Byron less,
>Because he knows not happiness?
>Ah, no ! tho' worlds condemn him now,
>Though sharp-tongued fame has sunk him low,
>The hapless wand'rer still must be
>Pitied, revered, adored by me.
>
>JANE BAILLIE WELSH.

But to be done with sentiment for the present, is not this a "d——d odd" affair of our handsome cousin's? He does not write as if anything was decided yet; on the contrary, his matrimonial fate seems to be poised in the scales of Fortune, with the most beautiful nicety. I can form no conjecture to which end the beam will incline. In the meantime he wishes me to come and keep house with *him* and Phœbe in Sussex-shire, that I may be present at his marriage, if it *does* take place, or comfort him if it does *not* —*comfort* the most bewitching man "in all England"! There *would* be an office!—if I were foolhardy enough to try it; but no! no! Mr. Baillie, I will stay at home here, and read my German books, which is dull work in comparison, but infinitely better for me.

The baskets are come, and have relieved my Mother from a great deal of anxiety about you. Present your Uncle with the *united* thanks of the family for the beautiful oranges. The hamper-looking thing *was* the parcel which my Mother spoke of; it contained *a jelly-glass and a butter-*

plate! which the Gilchrist was commissioned to buy for her. Moreover, I am desired to intimate to you, that you are to consider the *cake* from Templand the same as a cake from my mother, it having been made at her request; but this is a theorem which I do not pretend to demonstrate. Now, my dear, dear Angel Bessy, will you get for me at Wood & Small's, the first time you are in his neighbourhood, *Dolce concento* (Mozart), and *The Huntsman's Rest* (both of them Duets); *Rest, Warrior, Rest* (a song); also *The last Rose of Summer*, and *Roy's Wife of Aldivalloch*, with introductions and variations by Kiallmark.[7] If you do not like the commission, perhaps George Stodart will execute it for me. Did my Mother tell you that I had a letter from Lady Lenox? She is in a most interesting situation, James Baillie says. How d——d odd!

My kindest love to your Uncle, your Mother,

---

[7] A Swedish violinist (but born in England), who composed music for piano and violin. See Brown's *Biogr. Dict. of Musicians* (Paisley, 1886).

and the wee Lady,[8] in which my Mother joins. You can say to all the people who ask for me, that I desired particular remembrances to *them*. If it were not very late, and my pen very bad, I would write you another sheet, since I am about it. Good-night, dear. God bless you! Never forget me, and believe me always

    Your faithfully attached Friend,

       JANE BAILLIE WELSH.

---

[8] I do not know who this can be. This letter must (because of Goethe's autograph) be assigned to 1825: so it cannot be "the child" mentioned in Letter XVI., p. 115, who was not born till June of this year.

XV.

To Miss Stodart, 22 George Square, Edinburgh.

HADDINGTON,
11*th April* [Postmark, 1825].

MY DEAREST ELIZA,—

I do not think any one can accuse *me* of idle letterwriting, or you either, if I may judge from my own experience. Well "charity" (they say) "may exist without giving of alms,"[1] and friendship without the expressing of it by letters, so there is no great need for either apologizing or finding fault. I write to you when I have got anything to say; and am grateful for your letters when you are pleased to write them.

On the present occasion I have got something to say with a vengeance! Who do you think is living at the George Inn, and here every day? *Himself!* Mr. Benjamin B——! Had anybody

---

[1] "Though I bestow all my goods to feed the poor, . . . and have not charity" (1 Cor. xiii. 3). But here she states the converse.

told me some months ago that this thing would
come to pass, I believe I should have leaped over
the moon for very gladness; but "times are
changed, and we are changed in them."[2] Mr.
Benjamin B—— is become about the most disagreeable person on this planet, and *I* am become
—a fraction of a Philosopher! (This is no joke,
as I hope to convince you by-and-by. In the
meantime you may be as sceptical on the matter
as you please.) Mr. B.'s sojourn in this quarter
is very agreeable to me however, in one respect
—it affords me opportunities of repaying that
memorable bow with courtesies after a similar
fashion. Oh! it would have done your heart
good to have seen how I received him. It was
half dark when he came; my Mother and Catherine were working at the window, and I was
talking with Mr. Carlyle by the fireside; conceive my astonishment at so unlooked for an
apparition! *Himself* suddenly stood before me,

---

[2] *Tempora mutantur*, etc. The origin of this seems to
be, "*Omnia* mutantur, nos et mutamur in illis" (Matthias
Borbonius in the *Deliciæ Poetarum Germanorum*, i., 685).

all smiles and cordiality, and held out his hand.
I opened my eyes very wide, but my heart beat
no faster; I rose deliberately from my seat, and
made him such a decidedly ceremonious courtesy,
that I almost threw myself off my balance. He
looked—just as *I* did when he passed me on the
Waterloo Bridge; and I felt that I was revenged!
He was come, he said, to reside among us for
some time, to recruit his strength; he had been
ill—confined to bed for three months. It was
necessary that he should leave town, and his
acquaintance with us and Dr. Fyffe had induced
him to fix on Haddington as the place of his
retreat. How d——d odd! This curious an-
nunciation was addressed to my Mother. I
kept talking to Mr. Carlyle all the while about
the Peak of Teneriffe. Meanwhile the tea-kettle
commenced a song "*most musical, most melancholy,*"[3] which quite distracted my Mother's attention; she would not believe such sounds could

---

[3] " Sweet bird, that shunn'st the noise of folly,
Most musical, most melancholy ! "
Milton, *Il Penseroso*, 61, 62.

be produced by a mere tea-kettle. Mr. C. lifted it to convince her of the fact; he replaced it again. He tried it in various positions, but the kettle would not be prevailed upon. " It was chagrined," he said, and so was Mr. B——. He talked for two hours however, with a miraculous command of absurdity, and then departed, after promising to be exceedingly troublesome to us. I behaved to him then, and every time I have seen him since, in the most *pococurante* manner imaginable. I suspect he will soon be convalescent enough to return to the city. What a winding up of our romance! I would never have imagined that three years could have so metamorphosed any human being; from a frank-hearted, tasteful, promising young man, he is grown into a perfect personification of vanity and emptiness. *N'importe!* It is but one more bubble melted into thin air![4]

Speaking of bubbles, I do not go to London this

---

[4] " Are melted into air, into thin air."
Tempest, Act iv., Sc. 1.

season either, for reasons which I have not room to explain. It is not Mr. Irving's fault *this* time.[5] There was a letter from James Baillie the other night. "*His destiny is still undecided.*" Lord help him! He is certainly anything but wise, and his *innamorata* must be downright mad. Catherine G—— is not gone yet. She is quite a bug in her habits. There is no dislodging her.

Will you take the trouble to get some more music for me? Any time: I am in no hurry. I want *Tanti Palpiti* (with variations), *Ah perdona* (with variations), *The Carnival of Venice, Luther's Hymn, Theme from The Creation, Favourite Airs from Der Freyschütz, Christchurch Bells, Gli innocenti giuochi nostri;* and anything else you can recommend. Did you hear Miss Pola [?] had

---

[5] "It had been intended that Miss Welsh should pay Irving and his wife a visit in London as soon as they were settled. But Irving could not face the trial; he only hoped that a time might come when he might be able to face it. . . . 'Before another year [he wrote, apparently in 1823] I shall be worthy in the eye of my own conscience to receive you into my house and under my care, which till then I should hardly be.'"—Froude, *Thomas Carlyle*, A. i., p. 190.

got twins? What of Mrs. John? My kindest love to Bradie and your mother. Pray write soon like a good girl.

Ever affectionately yours,

JANE BAILLIE PEN[6] WELSH.

---

[6] "*Pen* was her little name there, from Paternal Grandfather's house, Penfillan, to distinguish her from the other *Welshes* of Walter's household" [Walter Welsh being her maternal grandfather].—Carlyle, *Reminiscences*, ed. Froude, ii., p. 101; ed. Norton, i., p. 78.

XVI.

To Miss Stodart, 22 George Square, Edinburgh.

Templand,
13*th August* [Postmark, 1825].

My dear, dear Angel Bessy,—

(Don't be frightened, there is no commission in the wind.) We were grieved to hear of your indisposition, and, as people have always most sympathy for the inflictions to which themselves are liable, we pitied you the more that your illness proceeded from bile. We hope however that the enemy is fairly overcome, and if so, my dear, you may sing a *Te Deum* for your deliverance. Think of me! I have been engaged in this same warfare, now, several years, and have never been able to work out more than a few weeks of truce. *Eh bien!* "ye shall become perfect thro' sufferings," says the Scripture[1]—a wholesome, comfortable doctrine for a bilious subject!

---

[1] The "ye shall become" is *not* "Scripture." See Hebrews ii. 10.

My life is passing on here in the usual alternating manner. One day I am ill, and in bed; the next, in full puff at an entertainment. On the whole, however, I feel myself better since I came here, than I had done for several months. What pains me most is that between headaches and visiting my *education* is completely at a stand. Every day my conscience reminds me of this in no gentle terms; calls me fool, and idler, and all sorts of injurious appellations: but I try to drown its clamours with promises of better behaviour in the time to come. And, after all, I am not *very* blameable on the score of idleness; it is in vain to think of toiling up the steep of knowledge with a burden of sickness on one's shoulders, and hardly less difficult for a young person with *my attractions* to lead the life of a recluse, however much I wish it. I dined at a club dinner the other day, consisting (not the dinner, but the company) of all the Justices (Just Asses) in the district with their wives. Mrs. ——, of B——, was among them, a d——d odd woman. She drank a bottle of wine during dinner, and was never a whit the worse for it. Speaking of "d——d odd"²—James Baillie's match is entirely broken off, and himself on the road to Scotland!! At least so says Captain Gordon, a friend of his sister's and wholesale gossip in these parts. There was a letter from the dear gentleman to my Mother since we saw you; but it was after the manner of the Lacedæmonians, and not a word of his *affairs* in it from beginning to end. Your Uncle will be glad to see some prospect of fingering the eighteen pounds. "O James, James, *vos discours ressemblent à des cyprès; ils sont grands et hauts, mais ne portent point des fruits.*"

I purpose going to Dumfries in a week or two on a visit to my Grandmother, and afterwards into—the lower district of Annandale to see³——the country. How is Bradie? Quite re-established, I hope. It is matter of great regret here that you and he cannot, or *will* not, come.

---

² Cf. Letter XIII., *note* 9, p. 97.

³ She went to visit the Carlyles at Hoddam Hill. See Froude, *Thomas Carlyle*, A. i., p. 308 ff.

And how is your half of the child?[4] Write to me *vite, vite.* The box arrived, but, alas! *not* in safety; in spite of your careful packing it was damaged in a great many places. *N'importe.* I should be but a young apprentice in philosophy if such things disturbed my equanimity much. I cannot tell you what has made me write so hurriedly and so ill, for I am not at all pressed for time—a restlessness in my mind I suppose. Love and a kiss to your uncle.

I am ever your faithfully attached friend,

JANE B. WELSH.

---

[4] "The child" was the first baby of Eliza's sister "Maggie" (see Letter XIII., *note* 10), and was named "Elizabeth" after her aunt and "Bradfute" after her aunt's uncle. She was a great deal with her aunt.

XVII.

To Miss Stodart, 22 George Square, Edinburgh.

Templand,
September [Postmark, *Sept.* 2nd, 1826].

Dear Eliza,—

You must think me *at least* graceless, perhaps downright uncivil; and, in truth, it is shameful that so fair a gift should be still to acknowledge. But this much I have to say, with all humility, in my own defence, that here, the source of offending lies in weakness of the flesh, not [un?]willingness of spirit, and the thanks, which I have been so overbackward to express, I have been anything but backward to feel.

Still I was sorry as much as glad about these ear-rings; for, while they pleased me as an emblem of friendly feelings on your part, of which, for reasons long and broad, I have of late been doubtful, I nevertheless wished them back again in Marshall's shop, when they glittered before my eyes under the form of a *mar-*

riage present. Not that I would keep the idea of my marriage out of mind. No, truly! it is fully more attractive for me now than ever—the greenest, sunniest spot in all my being. But marriage presents, I do think, are the most unreasonable species of *taxation* that could be devised. You remember Uncle Adam Ramsay's exposition of the matter to Miss Bell Black:

"There canna be a mair needless, daftlike thing, than to gie presents to a woman at the very height of mortal happiness. It is *she* rather should gie to puir single folk, that ha' na Major Waddely to set them up."

We got here last Monday—escaped alive from the thousand and one miseries of these last four weeks. I wonder that among all the evils deprecated in the Liturgy, no one thought of inserting *flitting*. Is there any worse thing? Oh no, no! From flitting, then, Good Lord, deliver us!¹ But while the way has been rough and

---

[1] Carlyle in a letter to his brother John on the occasion of the removal to Craigenputtoch (June 10th, 1828) has worked out this suggestion (unless, indeed, it originated

very fearful, it leads to "another and better world than this"—to a Heaven of truth and love and peaceful action, "a sober certainty of waking bliss,"[2] in which the temptation in the wilderness will be all forgotten, or remembered but as a troubled dream.

To you, however, I had best not proceed in this strain; your views of men and things "have little sympathy with mine." So that what I write for the finest sense in the world, you will perhaps throw in the fire as "*a pack o' nonsense.*"

Farewell then, my dear cousin. This most likely is the last letter you will receive from Jane Welsh;[3] but no change of name can work

---

with him): "From all packers and carpenters, and flittings by night or day, Good Lord, deliver us" (Froude, *Thomas Carlyle*, A. ii., p. 25). Prof. Norton has left out the part of the letter in which this occurs.

[2] "Such sober certainty of waking bliss."
Milton, *Comus*, 263.

[3] The marriage took place on October 17th. Mr. Froude (*ib.*, A. i., p. 364) says they were married in Templand church; Prof. Norton (*Early Letters*, ii., p. 366), that they were married in the bride's home, her grandfather's house at Templand, "according to the practice of the Scotch Church."

Seal used on Letters XI., XIV., XV. "Shandy," the dog, "a little Blenheim Cocker," is celebrated in Letter X., p. 9; Cf. Norton, *Early Letters of T. Carlyle*, I., p. 25, where a reference is made in a *note* to Carlyle's *Miscellanies, Works*, Library Edition, V., p. 27, *note*. It is there narrated how Shandy showed his appreciation of Sir W. Scott. The "J. C." I cannot explain.

in me the slightest change of heart—I mean towards those who are indeed my friends. My Mother, I suppose, will write to you in her own good time.

With kind regards to your Uncle,
I am always your affectionate
JANE B. WELSH.

—No: according to the practice which had become prevalent in Scotland: that is all.

XVIII.

[This undated note clearly goes along with the "Testimonial."]

To Revd. David Aitken, 35 George Street,
[Edinburgh.]

MY DEAR SIR,

I with great pleasure send you the "few lines"; and along with them my truest wishes for your success; wishes not ungenerous in themselves, as to *us* selfishly speaking your success can only be *loss*.

Let us know the moment anything is fixed: my wife is no less anxious than I.

Believe me ever,
Most truly your's,
T. CARLYLE.

[The following document is endorsed by Rev. D. Aitken, "Testimonial from Mr. Carlyle, Author of the *Life of Schiller* and *Translation of Wilhelm Meister*, etc." It is given here, as it shows how, even in this form of literature, Carlyle's individuality asserted itself.]

21 COMLEY[1] BANK,

17*th Feby.*, 1827.

OF Mr. Aitken's talent in the pulpit I can speak only by Report; the good testimony of which, however, every other indication tends to confirm. In private society, Mr. A. appears as a courteous, sincere, and highly intelligent man; of mild constant temper; of manners at once frank, cheerful, and gentlemanly: his conversation bespeaks a mind naturally clear, elegant, ingenious; now cultivated by sound temperate habits of thought, and in no ordinary degree, by manifold study and observation. In knowledge of Art, of Literature Ancient and Modern he has made distinguished acquirements: in German Literature especially, for which his long and varied residence in that country gave him peculiar

---

[1] In these letters of Carlyle, his spelling, use of capitals (though from his handwriting that is not always certain), and punctuation have been reproduced as nearly as possible. The place is, now at least, always spelt "Comely Bank." It is still, as in those days, in the country, although in Edinburgh.

opportunities, his knowledge, I believe, could be rivalled by few in Scotland, perhaps in Britain. His tastes also are still intellectual, and his habits regular and studious.

I have known Mr. A. only three months:[2] of his Moral Disposition, therefore, which only a long series of doings and forbearings can bring to the test, I have perhaps little right to speak; but I am *much* mistaken if Time do not prove it to be sterling, do not show him in all duties he may undertake acting with that mild judicious fidelity, and deep tho' unobtrusive regard to principle, which seems so accordant with his whole form of character. As a Clergyman, especially in an intellectual neighbourhood, he promises to be peculiarly suitable: for his religious persuasions seem to be at once earnest, unostentatious, and tolerant; and in point of

---

[2] Having made his acquaintance through Mrs. Carlyle, whose friend, Eliza Stodart, Mr. Aitken married in 1836. This testimonial was not written in vain. Mr. Aitken was presented in April of this year (1827) to the parish of Minto in Teviotdale by the patron, the Earl of Minto.

culture, and polish of mind, I can say without reserve that I have found few men in any profession, and certainly in his no one, that deserved to be compared with him.

THOMAS CARLYLE.

XIX.

To Revd. David Aitken, 39 George Street,
                    [*Edinburgh.*]

21. Comly¹ Bank,
                    29th June [1827].

My Dear Sir,—

I am very sorry that I missed you yesterday, and cannot now expect to meet with you till after our return from Dumfriesshire,² some weeks hence.

I had a letter from Dr. Julius,³ which I will show you; and a very brief Note from Goethe, intimating that he had sent (or rather on the

---

¹ *Sic.* See *note* 1 to Letter XVIII.

² Cf. Froude, *Thomas Carlyle*, A. i., p. 408: "In the summer [of 1827] he and his wife ran down for a short holiday at Scotsbrig [where his parents were], giving a few brief days to Templand [where her mother was living], and a glance at Craigenputtock. By August they had again settled at Comely Bank."

³ Dr. Julius was an acquaintance of Mr. Aitken, who had lived some time in Hamburg. Prof. Norton (*Early Letters of Thomas Carlyle*, ii., p. 321) describes him as " a widely travelled scholar and philanthropist."

17th of May was about "*nächstens*" to send) a parcel[4] hither, "*gleichfalls über Hamburg*." Now I know by experience how very negligent these Lieth[5] and Hamburg people are; nay, I am not without an opinion that the packet has already arrived, tho' on inquiring the other day at their Office I could get no information, the parcels being still all in the ship. Yet would it not be a proper vexation if a message of friendly tendency from "The Poet" were to be lost in such a despicable spot as the Lieth[5] Custom house? Knowing your experience in these matters, and your constant readiness to oblige, might I request that after your return you would some day make the necessary in-

---

[4] The parcel here expected must be that so joyfully received in August, containing wedding presents for "the valued marriage pair Carlyle" (as Carlyle translates in a letter to his mother), and a long letter, dated July 20th, given *in extenso* in German and English by Mr. Froude, *Thomas Carlyle*, A. i., pp. 399-405; and by Prof. Norton, *Correspondence between Goethe and Carlyle*, p. 13 ff. At page 11 will be found Goethe's brief note of May 17th, here referred to.

[5] Spelling apparently affected by much reading of German.

vestigations, and if unsuccessful in this instance, be afterwards on the outlook for this same precious *Sendung?* It would give us real pleasure to receive it in Dumfriesshire, and not the less that we owed it in part to your goodness. The Servant remains here, and knows our address.

With best regards from Mrs. C., I remain always,

My Dear Sir,
Very truly your's,
THOMAS CARLYLE.

XX.

[The removal to Craigenputtoch took place in May, 1828.]

To Miss Stodart, 22 George Square, Edinburgh.

CRAIGENPUTTOCH,

Monday [Postmark, *July* 29*th*, 1828].

" MY DEAR, DEAR ANGEL BESSY " ! ! !—

What a world of trouble is in these words announced to you! In fact, my tea is done, and my coffee is done, and my sugar, white and brown; and without a fresh supply of these articles my Husband would soon be done also. It might be got at Dumfries—but bad; and so I have bethought myself of your kind offer to do my commissions as of old, and find it come more natural for me to employ *you* in this way than another.

To proceed then, at once, to business, that so I may afterwards proceed with freedom to more grateful topics. Will you order for me at Polland's, in North Hanover Street (nearly opposite Miss Grey's), two stones of brown sugar at 8*d.*, and one stone, *very* brown, at 6½*d.*; as also a small loaf of white at 12*d.*, with five pounds of ground rice. Then, Angel Bess, you must not go home by the Mound, but rather along the Bridges, that you may step into the new tea establishment in Waterloo Place, and get me four pounds of tea at five and four pence per pound, two pounds at seven shillings, and two pounds of ground coffee at two shillings: this the Cockneys must be instructed to wrap up in strong paper and carry to Polland's, addressed to Mrs. Carlyle, Craigen etc., etc., and you will have the goodness to tell Polland beforehand that such a parcel will be sent to him to forward along with his sugar, and that he must pack the whole nicely up in a box and send it to the first Dumfries carrier, addressed to me, to the care of Mr. Aitken, Academy Street, Dumfries. Now one thing more, thou Archangel Bessy; you will pay these things (somewhere about 4 pounds, as I calculate) in the trembling hope of being repaid by the earliest opportunity, and unless it goes hard with me I will take good care that you are not disappointed. The truth is I have no five pound note to send you, and four small ones would make rather a bulky letter.[1] And here you may draw your breath, as I do mine; for I have nothing farther to trouble you with (except, on recollection, half a pound of Dickson's mustard), not even a longwinded apology for the trouble already given.

By this writing you will know that I have survived my astonishing change; and the talk about tea, etc., will show you that I even look hopefully into life. Indeed, Craigenputtoch is no such frightful place as the people call it. Till lately, indeed, our existence here has been made black with smoke; and confusion unspeakable was nearly turning our heads. But

---

[1] For each enclosure the full postage of a letter would have been charged. See Dr. G. Birkbeck Hill's *Life of Sir Rowland Hill*, i., p. 238.

we are beginning to get a settlement made at last, and see a distinct prospect of being more than tolerably comfortable. The solitude is not so irksome as one might think. If we are cut off from good society, we are also delivered from bad; the roads are less pleasant to walk on than the pavement of Princes Street, but we have horses to ride, and, instead of shopping and making calls, I have bread to bake and chickens to hatch. I read and work, and talk with my Husband, and never weary.

I ride over to Templand occasionally, and my Mother and Agnes Ferguson were here last week. They seemed content with the aspect of things, but my Mother is so confined at home now! She cannot be absent one night; and *that* home, I fear, is no peaceful place for *her*. I am sadly vexed about her; she is looking so ill and so unhappy.

You will write and tell me how all is going on at 22, and in Edinburgh generally. Dear Edinburgh! I was very happy there, and shall always love it, and hope to see it again often and often before I die. Will you give my kind regards to Mr. Simpson when you see him, and tell him I was well pleased to hear of his success? Remember us also to Mr. Aitken, and most affectionately to your Uncle. Do you know of any good habitmaker in Edinburgh (not very expensive)? I have got fine cloth for a habit, and am almost afraid to risk the making of it in Dumfries. Perhaps you could make inquiry for me, and let me know the charge, and whether a habit could be made from a pattern gown or pelisse. Grace Macdonald[2] is turning out a most excellent servant, and seems the carefullest, *honestest* creature living. She broke her arm soon after she came hither, but it is now almost quite strong again. I never miss a drop of "*broth*," and my linens are all entire.

My best wishes for Maggy and her new child, and "*I hope Mr. Dudgeon is quite well!*"[3] Letters from Germany and all parts of the earth

---

[2] Cf. *Reminiscences*, ed. Froude, ii., p. 149; ed. Norton, i., p. 80.

[3] Cf. Letter XIII., *note* 10, p. 97.

reach us here just as before. It is so strange to see "Craigenputtoch" written in Goethe's hand! But my paper is done.

Ever truly your friend,
J. W. CARLYLE.

XXI.

*To Miss Stodart, Mr. Bradfute's, 22 George
Square, Edinburgh.*

[*Oct.*, 1828.¹]

MY DEAR ELIZA,—

I know not whether the highly economical consideration of saving you double postage,² together with excessive occupation of late weeks, be reasonable apologies for not sooner paying my debt to you of money and thanks. At all events, I rely on your known *goodnature* to make the best of them.

You did not mention the amount of the said debt, but I calculated it was somewhere within five pounds, which I now take the opportunity of sending safely by Mrs. Jeffrey.

---

¹ Oct., 1828, was the date of the Jeffreys' *first* visit to Craigenputtoch, the second being in Sept., 1830 (Froude, *Thomas Carlyle*, A. ii., pp. 40, 125). If the £5 be, as is likely, in payment of the purchases caused by Letter XX., this letter must belong to the former date. Jeffrey is, of course, Francis Jeffrey of the *Edinburgh Review*.

² See Letter XX., *note* 1.

I meant to have added a long letter, having (which is not often the case with me) materials enough just at present to render a letter from Craigenputtoch tolerably interesting; but my good intention cannot be carried into effect at this time, the horses being come to take away our visitors earlier than we looked for, and a great bustle the usual consequence.

Excuse this being a scrawl then, till I send you a better specimen of my wits and my penmanship. And, if you please, acknowledge the receipt of it, that I may have no fear about its being miscarried. God bless you. Love to your Uncle.

Ever affectionately yours,
JANE CARLYLE.

CRAIGENPUTTOCH,
Friday morning.

XXII.

To Miss Stodart, 22 George Square, Edinburgh.

CRAIGENPUTTOCH,
21*st* November [Postmark, 1828].

MY DEAR ELIZA,—

Could you but see how it stands with me just at present, you would not be too much elated by this favour. For I am sitting here companionless, "like owl in desert,"[1] with nothing pressing to do, having learnt my daily task of Spanish,[2] and also finished a shirt—let me speak

---

[1] She seems to have in her mind both the versions of Psalm cii. 6, 7, in the "Scotch" metrical Psalms.

> "I like an owl in desert am,
> That nightly there doth moan;
> I watch, and like a sparrow am
> On the house-top alone."

> "The pelican of wilderness,
> The owl in desert I do match;
> And sparrow-like, companionless
> Upon the house's top, I watch."

[2] Cf. Froude, *Thomas Carlyle*, A. ii., pp. 48, 50; Norton, *Letters of Thomas Carlyle* [Second Series], i., p. 176.

truth, a nightshirt—I was making for my Husband, and it is come into my head as a resource from ennui that I should write somebody a letter; and thus, dear, all you have to be proud of is, that my choice of an object has fallen on *you*. I tell you this out of my natural love of plain dealing.

You would know what I am doing in these moors? Well, I am feeding poultry (at long intervals, and merely for form's sake), and I am galloping over the country on a bay horse, and baking bread, and improving my mind, and eating, and sleeping, and making, and mending, and, in short, wringing whatever good I can from the ungrateful soil of the world. On the whole, I was never more contented in my life; one enjoys such freedom and quietude here. Nor have we purchased this at the expense of other accommodations; for we have a good house to live in, with all the necessaries of life, and even some touch of the superfluities. "Do you *attempt* to raise any corn?" the people ask us. Bless their hearts! we are planning strawberry-banks, and shrubberies, and beds of roses, with the most perfect assurance that they will grow. As to the corn, it grows to all lengths, without ever consulting the public about the matter. Another question that is asked me, so often as I am abroad, is, how many cows I keep; which question, to my eternal shame as a housewife, I have never yet been enabled to answer, having never ascertained, up to this moment, whether there are seven cows or eleven. The fact is, I take no delight in cows, and have happily no concern with them. Carlyle and I are not playing farmers here, which were a rash and unnatural attempt. My brother-in-law[3] is the farmer, and fights his own battle, in his own new house, which one of his sisters manages for him.

In the autumn I had enough to mind without counting cows, the house being often full of visitors. There was Robert (my uncle) and Ann, a Mr. Graham of Burnswark,[4] Jeffrey, with wife

---

[3] Alexander Carlyle.

[4] For an account of this Mr. Graham, see *Reminiscences*, ed. Froude, i., p. 164; ed. Norton, ii., p. 81.

and child and maid and lap-dog, George and *his* wife, *our dear* Henry Inglis, and several others whom you do not know. And how on earth did Mr. Jeffrey get himself amused at Craigenputtoch? Why, in the simplest manner. He talked—talked from morning till night, nay, till morning again. I never assisted at such a talking since I came into the world, either in respect of quantity or quality.

Mrs. Richardson [5] is getting out a new edition of that weary book, and fitting out her daughter Willie for India; neither ware, I am afraid, will find a ready market.

John Carlyle is still in Germany. We looked for him home, but he has found that he could neither have peace in his lifetime, nor sleep quiet in his grave, had he missed studying six months in Vienna. Little Jane is gone back to Scotsbrig, where she could not be well spared, another sister being here with Alick. So that

---

[5] Probably the novelist, referred to in Norton, *Letters of Thomas Carlyle* [Second Series], i., p. 202; *Reminiscences*, ed. Froude, ii., pp. 34, 140; ed. Norton, i., p. 164; ii., p. 247.

Carlyle and I are quite by ourselves at present, moralizing together, and learning Spanish together, and in short, living in the most confidential manner imaginable. You never saw so still a house: we have just one servant (Grace Macdonald), and not even a cat in addition (for we find mousetraps answer much better). By the way, this Grace is just the cleverest servant I ever had occasion to know, and would be a perfect paragon in her line were it not for certain "second table" airs[6] about her, which without doubt she must have picked up at the Manners's.

My Mother dined here ten days ago, and stayed a night, her *second* and *longest* visit since we came. But she is of necessity much confined at home now, and also imagines the necessity to be greater than it is. You inquire if I will be in Edinburgh this winter. I think the chances

---

[6] "Second-table airs"; *i.e.* airs of an upper servant in a large house, where the upper servants have a table of their own, known as "the second table."

are about two to one that I shall. We are pressingly invited to spend some time with the Jeffreys; and Carlyle has agreed to go, provided he gets three papers, promised to the *Foreign Review*, finished by then. Should he be belated with these, he would have me go without him; but that I shall not dream of doing. It would be poor entertainment for one in Edinburgh or anywhere else to think one's husband was here in the desert *alone*, his stockings get[ting] all into holes, and perhaps even his tea running down.

Remember me in the kindest manner to your Uncle, and say to him that, if he will come and see us in the summer, the fatted calf shall be slain to make him welcome, to say nothing of lambs and poultry.

Remember me also to Sam, and to David Aitken when you see him. You talk of Mr. Simpson as an invalid. I hope he is recovered. Will you write to me soon? A letter from Edinburgh is such a treat to one here.

Carlyle is away in Annandale at present. His

eldest sister [7] has been ill for some time, and he is gone to see what can be done for her. I am afraid she is in a very bad way. Do write.

Ever affectionately yours,

J. W. CARLYLE.

---

[7] Margaret Carlyle (cf. Froude, *Thomas Carlyle*, A. ii., pp. 60, 61). She became better in the following summer, but died June 22nd, 1830 (*ib.*, pp. 109-113).

XXIII.

To Miss Stodart, Mr. Bradfute's, 22 George Square, Edinburgh.

CRAIGENPUTTOCH

[Postmark, *Dec.* 22*nd*, 1828].

MY DEAR ELIZA,—

"*Misfortunes seldom come single*"; so here is another letter for you, and of the most vexatious sort too, being all in the commission way. For, alas! dear, I can no longer hide the sad truth from myself, and as little would I conceal it from you, my early friend, that my tea and sugar are drawing fast to a close. And should a fall of snow take place in this state of things, blocking up the *passes,* and cutting off our imports—the idea is too horrible! But you will "do the impossible" to help me, for are you not "*obliging*" and "*goodnatured*" to a proverb? And yet if you had to begin the world again, I doubt whether (with your country cousins at least) you would cultivate so praiseworthy a reputation. Just see what it involves you in! Here must you tramp away to Polland's, to the Waterloo tea warehouse, the Register paper warehouse, the St. Andrew's Square china warehouse, and buy and arrange and dispatch, and all through no fault of yours, but because you have the merit of being the most obliging person of my acquaintance! Such a reward for virtue! but the Moralists say virtue is its own reward; and the Transcendentalists go a step further, and maintain that virtue must have no view to reward whatever, else it is no virtue but merely a cunning calculation of profit and loss. This last, I take it, is the opinion which would stand you in most stead on the present occasion.

Having preluded so long, it is time I were coming to the tune, which runs thus: Six pounds of tea (from the Waterloo company), at 5s. 4d., and two pounds of coffee. From Polland's, three stones of sugar, at 8d., and two stones at $6\frac{1}{2}d.$, also eight pounds of rice (whole). And here there is a sort of "*Da Capo*" to be performed, for in addition to what is already set down, you will have the goodness to get other two pounds of tea (of the same quality), and one other stone of 8*d.* sugar—packed up by themselves, being for a separate purpose. Then we are woefully off here as to pens and paper, which for people who live by writing are as essential as sugar and tea. So that it is earnestly desired, and (your "goodnature" being so notorious) even pretty confidently expected, that you will proceed to a certain paper-warehouse in Register Street, and procure us the supply as follows: Eight slips of post paper, wove, bluish, without any Bath stamp[1]—the same, in short, as this I am writing on, only a degree smaller (for me [? I], or rather my Husband, is "a great connoisseur in *paper*"). He used to buy such at the above mentioned place [at] about a halfpenny a sheet. I mention this to help you to the right sort—not to tie you down in the matter of a halfpenny. Secondly, three quires of *long* paper—twenty-four sheets each; this also to be *blue*, and a ragged edge no objection. The sort he used to buy was called "scrolling

---

[1] The stamp put by stationers on the top left-hand corner of the quarto letter paper known as "Bath post." She writes the word "bath."

paper," or broken paper, and cost between a *farthing* and a halfpenny a sheet. Now the Lord help you through this transaction, for, as you perceive, it is of the most delicate nature. A quarter hundred *made* pens of the best sort, and two sticks of red sealingwax, in addition to the above, will put us in a situation for holding correspondence with the home world all winter. And now comes my last want, which I am sure you will *welcome* with *your choicest mood*,[2] as his gracious Majesty did the youngest of the Misses Titler [? Tytler]—a brown earthenware coffee-pot, such as they sell in china shops for three and sixpence or four shillings; they are all made one shape, but of different sizes, and I would prefer the largest. For you must know that some mornings ago there came a letter to Grace Macdonald from some absent lover with " *hast* " on the outside, and Heaven knows what within—but things of moment, evidently, from the consequences—as she all at once bolted up from her peaceful

---

[2] Phrase of the court chronicler, I suppose, regarding something connected with George IV.'s visit. The name probably should be Tytler.

occupation of toasting bread for breakfast, and dashed the poor old coffee-pot with its precious contents on the kitchen floor—one more proof, if any such were wanting, that "accidents will happen in the best regulated families."[3]

Now as to the packing of these things. I am really, without any blarney, seriously vexed to put you to so much trouble, but I see no other way for it except that you should pack them at your own house in some box of my Mother's (if you have such a thing), or of your own (and it will be returned by the first opportunity), and sending [? send] it from thence to the Dumfries carrier (charging the porterage, etc., to my account, if you would ever have me to employ you again), addressed as formerly to Mr. Aitken's, Academy Street. For the last supply was sent off by Polland's in the thinnest of sacks, so that had it rained, as it does almost continually at present, it must have been entirely spoiled by the way.

---

[3] This same disaster is recounted by Carlyle in a letter of Dec. 11th to Mr. Henry Inglis.—Norton, *Letters of Thomas Carlyle* [Second Series], i., p. 180.

And should I find my sugar all melted, and the paper all blotted, and the coffee-pot broken, I might be tempted to do some desperate thing that would haunt your conscience to the end of your life! You will do this then for the love you bear me, or at all events for the love of doing a good action; and you will believe that, if our situations were exchanged, I would do as much for you in return? We have resolved on deferring our visit to Edinburgh until the spring,[4] when it will be in all respects more convenient. Why do you not write?

My kindest regards to your Uncle. I shall remain some shillings in your debt, but always

Affectionately yours,

JANE WELSH CARLYLE.

---

[4] The visit to Edinburgh apparently did not take place till autumn. Carlyle, writing in August [?], 1829 (Norton, *Letters of Thomas Carlyle* [Second Series], i., p. 203), says: "It seems to be settled that we are to go and see Edinburgh, and the Jeffreys, so soon as they return; which will not be for six weeks or so." See, also, the beginning of Mrs. Carlyle's next letter (XXIV.).

XXIV.

Miss Stodart, 22 George Square, Edinburgh.

CRAIGENPUTTOCH,

11*th November* [Postmark, 1829].

MY DEAR ELIZA,—

You know, or might know, that I rarely avail myself of *opportunities,* choosing to write as the Quakers preach, only when the spirit moves me. But in the present instance the opportunity and the inspiration are come together—a happy chance! which makes *you* richer by eightpence halfpenny, money saved being money won.

Well, it is all over (the visit to Edinburgh I mean), and we are gradually subsiding into our old still-life—no longer "*in the midst of everything that is intellectual and delightful,*" but in the midst of a pretty extensive peat-moss. Which mode of living is best? In the sun or in the shade? I declare I cannot tell; my mind seems to have a peculiar knack of adapting itself to either. I liked Edinburgh last time as well as I did at sixteen (you know how well that was), and I cried as much at leaving it; yet, returned to our desert, it affrighted me only the first day. The next day it became tolerable, and [the] next again positively pleasant. On the whole, the mere outward figure of one's place of abode seems to be a matter of moonshine in the long run. You learn (if you are not an entire goose) to pronounce it, once for all, "*particular neat*," or, as it may happen, particular *un*neat; and then naturally betake yourself into some other train of speculation. The only thing which makes one place more attractive to me than another is the quantity of *heart* I find in it; it is this which, in default of a self-dependent mind, "can make a Heaven of Hell" for me, "a Hell of Heaven."[1] I was happy in Edinburgh, because you, and your Uncle, and the Jeffreys, and one or two more

---

[1] "The mind is its own place, and in itself
Can make a Heaven of Hell, a Hell of Heaven."
Paradise Lost, i. 253.

were so friendly towards us, so *very* kind! And now I am happy here also, because Carlyle always likes me best *at home*, wherever that happens to be. And then the kindness which I experienced among you, and felt so gratifying, is not a *fixture* to be made over to the next comer, on my removal, but *personal property*, to be carried away, and treasured up, and enjoyed here in the moors of Dunscore, or wherever else I please, so that the best charm of Edinburgh is still present with me; though its pavements and ashlar houses, its fine companies and "*fine wines*" are exchanged for sheep-tracks, blocks of granite, solitariness, and spring water.

Mr. Moir stayed only two days with us, and both were rainy; but he made his sketches for Goethe nevertheless.[2] Carlyle took him to Temp-

---

[2] Cf. *Reminiscences*, ed. Froude, ii., p. 154; ed. Norton, i., p. 85. "The *Sketch* of Craigenputtock [two sketches sent to Goethe at his request, and engraved for the German translation of Carlyle's *Life of Schiller*] was taken by G. Moir, Advocate (ultimately Sheriff, Professor, etc., 'little Geordie Moir,' as we called him), who was once and no more with us." George Moir was Professor of "Rhetoric and Belles

land on his way back, where they stayed all night; and my Mother, with her characteristic liberality, presented him with a bag of oatmeal!! It was their first interview, and I think little Moir will remember it.

Indeed this "raising not of *black mail*, but *white meal*" (as he expressed it), must have gratified him not a little. I question if he ever made so successful a descent into the country in his life. I had a letter from her this morning, wishing me over; and I purpose going the first dry day.

The gloves and thistle and picture frames arrived all safe, and the umbrella, which has been in constant action ever since; but I was disappointed that you did not send a line, just to say you were sorry I was gone. However I do trust you will write soon, for we must *not*

Lettres" ("Rhetoric and English Literature" is the title now) in Edinburgh University from 1835 to 1840. He gave up the chair to become Sheriff of Ross-shire. He was afterwards Professor of Scots Law from 1863 to 1865 (Sir A. Grant, *The Story of the University of Edinburgh*, ii., pp. 359, 375).

lose sight of each other again. I never loved you better than I do at this moment, never half so well; for, as I told you in Edinburgh, my affections are not getting feeble with my increasing years, but are rather, now for the first time, unfolding themselves into right activity.

And Carlyle too loves you more than you are aware. He has talked over and over again of your and your Uncle's kindness to us while we stayed with you, for not one of your unceasing attentions were lost on him for all that he looks so impenetrable.

I have hung up Sandy Donaldson[3] over the mantlepiece in my own room, whence he looks down upon me with the most bewitching simper night and morning. The first time I had occasion to dress in his presence I found myself unconsciously stepping behind the curtains. Carlyle could hardly keep his hands off him at first, and declared "there he should not

---

[3] Mr. Donaldson of Sunnybank, Haddington, I suppose. The family are often referred to in *Letters and Memorials*.

hang"; but he now professes to be rather *wae*[4] for him (he is so exceedingly ugly) and has taken up a sort of patronage of him. And so God bless you, dear. A kiss to your Uncle.

JANE W. CARLYLE.

My kindest regards to both.—T. C.[5]

---

[4] *Wae*, i.e. sorry, grieved, as in Burns's *Address to the Deil*, "I'm wae to think upo' yon den"; and in the story told in *Letters and Memorials*, i., p. 260, *note* 1, about the man who said to another, "I's wae for you," and met the retort, "Damn ye, be wae for yersel."

[5] Postscript by Carlyle.

XXV.

To the Revd. David Aitken, of Minto by Melrose.[1]

CRAIGENPUTTOCH, DUMFRIES,
21st *December*, 1829.

MY DEAR SIR,—

If this letter ever reach Minto Manse, you will have little cause to rejoice in the arrival; for it will only cost you postage, and give you trouble.

You must know I have partly engaged with certain London Booksellers to produce some sort of *Historical View of German Literature*,[2] for some "Cabinet Library" or other; and am busy

---

[1] Carlyle's mistake, instead of "Hawick." See *P.S.* to next letter, p. 167.

[2] This projected *History* never appeared. The materials collected for it were used by Carlyle for his first course of lectures (Froude, *Thomas Carlyle*, B. i., p. 98) and in various articles for the *Edinburgh*, *Foreign Quarterly*, and *Westminster Reviews*, afterwards published in the *Critical and Miscellaneous Essays*. See the "Bibliography" appended to Dr. Garnett's *Life of Carlyle*.

at this very time in laying in all manner of provision for that undertaking. It is to be in four volumes, and the first should appear in spring. Whittaker's people[3] have promised me seas and mountains in the way of furnishing Books: but in the meanwhile nothing whatever has come to hand; nay, I know such promises, at any rate, too well to slacken my endeavours after help elsewhere.

If in your Collection there is anything that you can spare for me, I know it will be lent me with your old frankness. There is one little series of yellow-coloured volumes, containing a short *Life* and some Specimen (one in each volume) of the chief German writers, in their order; Hans Sachs, Santa Clara, etc.,

---

[3] Does this imply that Whittaker was the publisher who was to bring out the work? In 1831 Carlyle speaks of Dr. Lardner's offer to publish it in his *Cabinet Cyclopædia* as a new proposal (Norton, *Letters of Thomas Carlyle* [Second Series], i., pp. 379, 389). In 1839 he writes, "The unfortunate *Cabinet Library* Editor . . . broke down" (*Correspondence of Carlyle and Emerson*, i., p. 228), referring apparently to this first scheme.

etc., I recollect having read : the whole of these little volumes would be highly convenient for me. I suppose you have no special Life of Ulrich Hutten, nor any considerable portion of his Works? I am also gleaning everything about Luther, Sebastian Brandt, etc., etc. Bouterweck's and Eichhorn's Histories I expect from the South. The last three volumes of the Conversations-Lexicon (from "Schubart," where my own last *Lieferung* stops) I would also ask, if it were not a shame. Unhappy Conversations-Lexicon! It has taken twenty months to come from München; and that fraction of it is still wandering the wide world!

Now if you could take those little yellow volumes, with whatever else you think useful, and can want for six or seven months; and have them forwarded to your worthy namesake "Sam. Aitken," of Bank Street, he will send them on to me without delay. At all events, let me hear from you, at great length; and fail not to give me your counsel, and *geprüftes Wort* in this unspeakable enterprise. I will tell Mr. Aitken to wait for your packet about eight days; and after that to transmit what he may have got; for the London Books also are to be consigned to him: the Minto stock, should any hindrance have occurred, may follow at any other time. But do not fail to write, however it may be: the Post will convey your tidings, and we will warmly welcome them, now as well as afterwards.

We rejoice to learn in general that you prosper in Minto; and often we hoped last summer that some lucky wind would blow you into Nithsdale, and up to these moors for one happy week. Alas, for the Wednesday-nights![4]

---

[4] In a letter of 1827, from 21 Comely Bank, Carlyle writes to his brother Alexander: "We give no dinners and take none; and by the blessing of Heaven design to persist in this course as long as we shall see it to be best. Only to some three or four chosen people we give notice that on Wednesday nights we shall *always* be at home, and glad if they will call and talk for two hours with no other entertainment but a cordial welcome and a cup of innocent tea" (Norton, *Letters of Thomas Carlyle* [Second Series], i., p. 29). But apparently coffee also was provided for those who preferred it and did not find tea "innocent."

Alas, and alackaday! But Time goes on his stern course, and treads our little card-castles into shivers, and the Past will not give up its dead!—Surely you will come *this* Spring, and let us recal old times. Write, and say that you are no craven, but stand to your word.

We live in a strange, quite original position here, environed with "solitude and primeval Nature." To-night there is [snow][5] and black haze, and deepest silence all round for miles; but within is a blazing fire, and a cap-making Wife, and Books and Paper, and Time and Space to employ worthily or unworthily. Come and see, if you would understand it.

My Brother John returned last spring with wonderful accounts of Munich and Vienna and Strasburg and Paris, and the other phenomena of this Earth. He is gone two weeks ago to settle in

---

See end of this letter; and cf. *Reminiscences*, ed. Norton, i., p. 79.

[5] The paper is torn. The word may be "frost," but I think the fragment of the first letter is more like one of Carlyle's *s*'s.

Warwick where some friends of his and mine hold out fair offers. I have not heard of him yet.

Did you read Sir W. Hamilton[6] on Cousin's Metaphysics in the last *Edinburgh Review*? And what inferences are we to draw from it? Pity that Sir W. had not the gift of delivery! He has real knowledge on those matters; but all unsorted, and tumbled topsyturvy like a "bankrupt stock."

If you ever see Dr. Brewster,[7] pray assure him that he is not forgotten here; but that best wishes for him dwell in the Nithsdale wilderness, which is a strange residence for them.

---

[6] In 1833, during the Edinburgh visit, he writes: "The best man I see here, indeed the only man I care much about, is Sir William Hamilton; in whom alone of all these people I find an earnest soul, an openness for truth: I really think him a genuine kind of man" (Norton, *Letters of Thomas Carlyle* [Second Series], ii., p. 82. Cf. Froude, *Thomas Carlyle*, A. ii., pp. 329, 332, 343, 346). The article on Cousin is republished in Hamilton's *Discussions*.

[7] Afterwards Sir David Brewster and Principal of Edinburgh University. At this time he was still editing the *Edinburgh Encyclopædia*, begun in 1808, and not completed till 1830.

Your ancient "Wednesday-night" hostess here would skip for joy to make you coffee once more! She bids me send you her affectionate regards; she too would fain hear from you soon. Believe me ever,

Most sincerely your's,

T. CARLYLE.

XXVI.

To the Revd. David Aitken, of Minto by Melrose.

CRAIGENPUTTOCH,
26*th January*, 1830.

MY DEAR SIR,—

Your very kind Letter arrived here in due time; and shortly afterwards, the Packet it had announced, containing (if I have counted rightly) 16 volumes of *Rassmann*, 6 of the *Conversations-Lexicon*, with *Gleim* and *Koch*, all of which were highly welcome, and shall be properly cared for, and, I hope, turned to use in their season. No less valuable to me were your friendly offers of farther help; and your counsels and indications, which agree perfectly with my own views on the matter, so far as I yet have any views. That your good wishes may be turned forthwith into good deeds, I purpose applying to you again; and often, as I proceed in my little enterprize, which for me will be great enough.

The "History of German Literature," for which I only bargained finally last Wednesday, is to consist of Four small volumes, and ought to include whatever, at this epoch, is most interesting to us of England in the past and present condition of that wide province; not, of course, a minute chronicle-detail, of the Eichhorn fashion, for which neither I nor my readers are in any measure qualified; but views of the more prominent and, as it were, universal features (*welt-historisch*) of that huge subject; wherein it will be most of all important that they *be* real views, seen into with my own eyes (tho' from this distance), not hallucinations, and hearsays, and *Trugbilder*, seen into with other people's eyes, perhaps never seen into at all. I propose, like Rabelais' Ram, to *commencer par le commencement*;[1] not omitting even the *Mährchen* of pri-

---

[1] Mr. George Saintsbury suggests that Carlyle has mixed up the Ram of Dindenault (Rabelais, book iv., ch. vi.-viii.) with a passage in Antoine Hamilton's *Le Bélier*, where the giant Moulineau says to the Ram, who was beginning to tell a story in the middle, "Bélier, mon ami, si tu voulais bien commencer par le commencement, tu me ferais plaisir" (*Œuvres* ii., p. 153; ed. 1812). The story is translated into English. See Count Hamilton's *Fairy Tales* (Bohn's series), p. 474.

meval centuries, about Etzel and Dietrich of Bern; still less the *Heldenbuch* and *Nibelungen Lied*, or the *Minnesänger*, or *Meistersänger*, or any other picturesque or characteristic aspect of the German mind. Judge then if I shall welcome your antiquarian collections, whether printed or manuscript, in this my almost total dearth of information on those matters! Pray let me have *all* that you can spare: the *Nibelungen*; Tieck's *Schwabischen Zeitalter*,[2] of which I understand the Preface is highly instructive; the *Epistolæ obscurorum Virorum, Reinike*[3] *de Vos*; and everything else that your charity can furnish. Flögel's *History of Comic Literature* I *must* contrive to get: the era of the Reformation will of course be one of the very highest "culminations" of the subject; and, indeed, on other grounds I have long been striving (with little success) to represent it to myself under all possible points of view. If *Flögel* cannot be had in Edinburgh, I have little hope of

---

[2] This, of course, should be *Schwäbisches Zeitalter*.
[3] Should be *Reineke*.

it in London, and must send for it to Germany, were this frost once away. Koch seems to be an excellent person of his kind: I fear you have not the second volume, which I find was published two years later, and completes the poetical department of his task. Eichhorn, whose terrific farrago now lies beside me, is surely *the* most unspeakably stupid man of Learning that has lived in modern centuries: "like an ass whose back with ingots bows,"[4] he is no richer than if he carried pot-metal, and cannot bring himself the smallest necessary. I hope and trust, Bouterweck will prove a little better.

You perceive, I am casting myself altogether on your discretion; leaving you not only to provide me with help, but to judge also what help I shall most need. Since you have "unrolled your pack" before me in such courteous style, I can only request you to choose for me, by your own skill; with the assurance, hardly necessary in this case, that *too much* can produce no incon-

---

[4] *Measure for Measure*, Act iii., Sc. 1.

venience, and too little may cost me serious trouble. If, besides the Works you have mentioned, regarding the Reformation-period, and prior (to which, if it were not shameless to ask them, your own Notes and Extracts would be a valuable accession), you can think of anything else that would prove instructive, I shall receive it, and employ it, with true thankfulness. *Luther*, I think, must terminate the first volume, before whom come all the Fablers and Satyrists, and Swabian Minne-singers, and Nürnberg Master-singers, a motley horde which I do pray devoutly I had marshalled into something like clear order. A work, or even the name of a good work, on the *Meistersängerei* would be a special blessing to me: I can find none but one of Grimm's, which I fear will be but a shallow one. Do you know Docen's and Hagen's *Hist. of German Poetry*? I have seen it in the Edin^r. College Library, but read only a few pages of it. Or Büsching's *Hans Sachs*, and whether there is a *Life* prefixed to it?

But I must draw bridle here; for the Paper is exhausted, to say nothing of your Patience.

You will have the "luxury of doing good"[5] for your reward of all this trouble; other reward I dare not for the present promise you. Alas, I am a sorely straitened man! This same *History*, the first volume of it, was to go to press in April, and here am I with empty bookshelves, and head "to be let unfurnished!" But guild-brethren will prove kind, in the loan of tools, which our brave *Speditions-handler*[6] of Bankstreet will faithfully forward me; and for the head, we may sweep if we cannot garnish it. So *allons!*

The Brown cann,[7] or a perfect resemblance of it, is still here; and will hold itself bound to perform, in first order, for an old friend. You positively must not let this summer slip without an expedition hither. The scene, it is true, belongs to the class of Bog and Hill scenery, and has little but heath and whinstone and peat-pits

---

[5] "And learn the luxury of doing good."
    Goldsmith, *Traveller*, 22.

[6] Should be *Speditionshändler*.

[7] Has a suggestion of the German *Kanne* (Mid. Eng. *canne*), made him spell thus? He means the coffee-pot evidently. See Letter XXIII., p. 145.

to recommend it: nevertheless, it *is* a scene; under the everlasting vault, and has two hearts that honestly take interest in you, and always remember you with affection. Consider this, and fulfil your purpose. Meanwhile, write to me when[ev]er you have leisure: nay, for the present you have real " business " to write on. Also, be careful of your health in these wild winter months; and be well when I come to Minto, which I mean to do the very first time I am in Edin^r. Mrs. Carlyle bids me " be sure to send her love." I remain always,

Most sincerely yours,
T. CARLYLE.

You do not mention your Post-town, and I see *Hawick* on your Letter. However, *Melrose* found you last time, *so wollen wir bey'm*[8] *Alten bleiben.*

Mr. Aitken will probably send me a Parcel on Tuesday week,—to be here on Wednesday, which is our market and packet day: of *posts* we have one other on Saturday, and that is all.

---

[8] Would be written *beim* now.

XXVII.

To Miss Stodart, 22 George Square, Edinburgh.

CRAIGENPUTTOCH,

5th February [Postmark, 1830].

DEAREST ELIZA,—

This has been the unluckiest new year to me! Every day some Job's-post or other tempts me to curse my stars! It began with the death of my pig—my sweet, wise, little pig, who was the apple of my eye; he got a surfeit one evening, and next morning I was pigless! and just when my long-cherished hopes of him were approaching their fulfilment, and a few weeks more would have plumped him out into such delicate bacon! So the glory of this world passeth away![1] On the back of this severe family-affliction followed a disaster occasioned by a quite opposite cause, being the consequence, not of overfeeding, but

---

[1] *Sic transit gloria mundi*, the beginning of a "sequence" in the Roman Church, and said to have been formerly used at the inauguration of the popes (Bohn's *Dict. of Latin Quotations*). But probably 1 Corinthians vii. 31 was in her mind: "For the fashion of this world passeth away."

pure starvation: a stranger cat under the pangs of famine rushed wildly into our larder one day, making straight in the direction of a beefsteak; and, before you could bless yourself, snack went the steak, and smash went a *corner-dish*, which you know was as bad as if the whole four corner-dishes had been broken, or at least a pair of them. And, alas! this was only a beginning. This smash, it seemed, was but a signal for the breakage of all the crockery, glass, and china about the house. For now Nancy became as it were suddenly possessed with a demon of destruction which shivered everything she laid hands on; nay, the supper-tray, with all its complement of bowls, plates, etc., etc., she "*soopit ower wi' her tails*"![2] one fell *soop!* But already I must have filled your eyes with tears, and will not tax your sympathy with a detail of *all* my grievances; indeed, one sheet would not hold them. Only attend to the last, which you must help me to remedy, being in truth the main cause of my writing again so soon.

---

[2] *I.e.* swept over with the tail of her petticoats.

Last week we were despatching a boxfull of books to Sam to be transmitted to their various owners in Edinburgh. None of our own people being "at *the* town"[3] that Wednesday, it was entrusted to the Carrier, who naturally was charged *to pay it;* but, our ill luck pursuing us even in this small matter, the carrier either misunderstood or proved oblivious; and so the package was despatched, with all its charges to be defrayed at Bank Street. Now, tho' intrinsically considered the damage done by this mistake be trifling, yet you will understand how one should find it abundantly vexatious; and I beseech you to explain to Mr. Aitken how the omission, which must have appeared to him so singularly inconsiderate, occurred, and to charge him (by his Lady's love or whatever he values most) to place this, with every expense which these book commissions cost him, to Carlyle's account. If he does not, we shall not be able to apply to him with any freedom, and I doubt if in all Edinburgh we could find another as helpful.

---

[3] Dumfries.

And now, contrary to my usual practice, "I must plant a remark" or two on the weather. It is well we have meat and fire "*within ourselves*" (as Mrs. Roughhead used to say), otherwise we should live in hourly apprehension of being snowed up, and consequently starved to death without even the mournful alternative of "*eating our own children.*" Oh for a sight of the green fields again, or even the black peat-moss—anything rather than this wide waste of blinding snow! The only time when I can endure to look out (*going* out is not to be dreamt of) is by moonlight, when the enclosure before the house is literally filled with hares, and then the scene is really very picturesque, the little dark forms skipping and bounding over the white ground so witch-like! A still more novel spectacle exhibited itself the other day at broad noon. Seven blackcocks, "as *fine* (or perhaps finer) *as ever stepped the streets of Greenock,*"[✝] came run-

---

[✝] Cf. *Letters and Memorials of Jane Welsh Carlyle*, ii., p. 335. "I should have been as astonished to meet *him* in Kirkcaldy as to meet Tiger Wull's 'finest blackcock that

ning down the wood to within a few yards of the door. Such are the pleasing varieties of life here. You will allow they are extremely innocent.

Carlyle inquired if I had sent his love the last time, and charges me to remember it now. We speak of your Uncle and you over our evening fire both often and kindly. My kindest regards are with you both. My Grandfather continues much the same. God bless you!

Always affectionately yours,
JANE W. CARLYLE.

A good new year, and many of them.—T. C.

---

ever stepped the streets of Greenock'!'" On which passage Carlyle's annotation runs: "'Teeger Wull,' Tiger Will—William Dunlop, a well known cousin of hers, one of the strangest men of his age, with an inexhaustible sense of fun. One friend promised another (according to Wull) 'the finest blackcock that,' etc." But may there not be a further joke, hidden behind the mere incongruity of this remark? A correspondent points out that "blackcoats" (*i.e.* ministers, clergymen) might easily or wilfully be mispronounced "blackcocks." But perhaps "an inexhaustible sense of fun" is needed to *see* this joke, whatever it is.

XXVIII.

To Miss Stodart, 22 George Square.

CRAIGENPUTTOCH,

Day of the month unknown.

[End of Dec., 1830, or Beginning of Jan., 1831 ?]

DEAREST ELIZA,—

It is almost worth while to have a sore throat "*at a time*"[1] to rouse lethargic friends into naturality. I had quite lost all expectation of hearing from you, and what is more, lost all acquaintance of your handwriting, so that I could not conjecture from the address on your letter from whom it came. The seal I thought I had seen before, but could not possibly recollect where; and when I "*took a peep into the inside*" my perplexity was only increased. "*New admi-*

---

[1] *I.e.* occasionally (cf. p. 30). Mr. Froude mentions "a violent sore-throat" "at the close of Dec.," 1830 (*Thomas Carlyle*, A., ii., p. 67).

nistration," "*Duke of R*——" "*damnable heresy*,"[2] —who *could* it be at all? At length, to my great relief (for I could find no signature) my eye lighted on a wee, unforgetable "*Bradie*," and then I was as glad as might be, and astonished at my own stupidity. It is a real hardship that you will not write oftener; it is only through *your* letters that any tone of the old time ever reaches me, all the rest of my young companions, if they have not got new faces, having at least got new dialects. And then you have such plenty of interesting matter lying on all hands. If you were in *my* place, you would have more excuse, who have to produce letters as the silk-worm spins, all out of my own inside.

We have been very solitary for a long while, our only visitors are now and then a stray packman, and the last of these pronounced the place

---

[2] Lord Grey's ministry came into office in Nov., 1830, and included the Duke of Richmond, as Postmaster-general. Eliza Stodart was probably quoting her uncle, who may have used the phrase "damnable heresy" about the Reform agitation.

"altogether *heathenish*," so there is no hope of our being favoured with *his* company another time. Nevertheless, I keep up my heart. There is nothing like a good bit of pain for taking the conceit out of one. Had I been newly returned from Edinburgh, my thoughts still wandering on the mountain tops of vanity, it is probable I should have found life here, in this grimmest of weather, almost intolerable; but being newly recovered from a sore throat, I am quite content beside a good fire, with a book or work, and the invaluable capacity of swallowing, though the desert around looks the very headquarters of winter, and our knocker hangs a useless ornament.

My Grandfather was no worse when my Mother wrote last week; and her luck seemed to be taking a favourable turn: she had got a visitor, than whom "*no sweeter ever crossed a threshold.*" I mean to spend a week with her so soon as I am able to ride; but I am not *quite* well yet—at least, I am still wearing signals of distress, a nightcap and shawl—that, partly, I confess, from a secret persuasion that these equipments render my appearance more interesting. But, Mercy! here is a dark night come upon me, and a box has yet to be packed with which a man has to ride six miles thro' the snow. I will write you at more length another time; and in the meanwhile this will show my good intentions. God bless you, dear. A kiss to your Uncle.

In breakneck haste,
Your affectionate friend,
JANE W. CARLYLE.

XXIX.

[If "the late political changes" are the same as those referred to in Letter XXVIII., this letter belongs to 1831. If the change be only the Duke of Wellington taking office in October, 1828, it would have to be assigned to 1829. Carlyle (*Reminiscences*, ed. Froude, ii., p. 156; ed. Norton, i., p. 87) says the death of Esther of Carstamin occurred "one of our early winters [*i.e.* at Craigenputtoch]." This might seem to suit 1829 better; but 1831 was before the winter in London, and might therefore be so described. On the whole I prefer the later date; although, indeed, Eliza Stodart was, if possible, less likely to "go into office," even as "Court-Marmalade-Maker," under a Whig than under a Tory administration. She was brought up among Tories, though she married a Whig. For the marmalade-making, cf. Postscript to Letter V., p. 27.]

To Miss Stodart, 22 George Square, Edinburgh.

CRAIG O' PUTTA,

16*th January* [1831?].

"THE Lord bless thee," Eliza!¹

It is long since I got your letter, and it was also very long before I got it.

---

[1] Edward Irving's salutation. Cf. Norton, *Letters of*

Never say I was not ready to correspond at any rate you pleased. Your pleasure seems to be a very languid rate; and so be it!

I find myself in tolerable health, and sound mind. How do *you* find yourself? Have the late political changes any way affected *your* destiny? Have you gone into office, my dear friend?

The Edinburgh news travel hither so slowly —often *viâ* London—that you may even have been appointed *Court-Marmalade-Maker* without my hearing a word of the matter. Jeffrey writes faithfully and fully—no one else in Edinburgh; but his local information never passes the garden walls of Craig-crook.[2] *You* used to send me "sundry news of every kind," and often has a letter from you recovered me out of dolefullest dumps. But, alas! you have either lost your talent, or hidden it in a napkin! A letter from you now-a-days is as rare a curiosity as yon

---

Thomas Carlyle [Second Series], i., p. 156: "Cant and enthusiasm are strangely commingled in him: . . . in place of ordinary salutation [he] bids 'the Lord bless you.'"

[2] Jeffrey's house, near Edinburgh.

big Moth which my Mother presented to the Museum. Mercy, what think you is come of it? Our Mother was shabbily used about that "*little Eagle*"[3] of hers. I remember she had engaged to the Postmaster at Fort Augustus that he should see his windfall in the newspapers, and was making sure of at least *one* silver ticket of admission, which would enable her, without the charge of half-a-crown, to regale herself with a view of the "valuable addition presented by Mrs. Welsh," as often as she pleased. The Professor, I think, merely "wondered what the *Moth* was doing so far north at that season of the year"; on which somebody else suggested a second wonder, "what Mrs. Welsh was doing so far north at that season of the year." And so the whole Moth-speculation died a natural death, and only the bottled up Moth-Eagle, or Eagle-Moth, remains (if indeed it do remain), a memorial to coming time of Moth-

---

[3] My friend Mr. E. B. Poulton suggests that it was probably a large hawk-moth.

inquisitiveness, female philanthropy, and professorial ingratitude.

But where were we? I was saying that a letter from you was a rare curiosity, and the words, Heaven knows how, instantaneously brought back the image of that ill-fated little being which has not been once in my head these half dozen years. Well! it is vain to reason with you further on the subject of writing, for you will not hearken to the voice of the charmer, charm she ever so wisely!

I should like to spend another week with you, and renew my years, as in my last visit; not that I am looking any older than when you saw me. On the contrary, notwithstanding my prediction that I should fall off rapidly after twenty, I keep my looks surprisingly well. An old Irish packman met me riding alone the other day, and modestly insinuated that I should buy an almanack of him.

"By no means."

"But I have travelled all day, Lady, and got nothing to pay my lodging!"

"Well, for God's sake, there's a penny to you."

"Thank you, *young* Lady—thank you most kindly; and "—his gratitude and his voice mounting higher and higher, till they reached the pitch of enthusiasm—"and the Lord send you a Husband according to your heart!"

"Amen, friend."

From which passage one may infer one of two things—either that an Irish packman thought me too youthful looking to be already provided with a Husband; or that he conceived the provision of a Husband incompatible with galloping over the country *alone*. I saw in one of your letters to my Mother that you were living very quietly; yet gentlemen bring you nice nosegays. We, I imagine, are yet quieter; a gentleman either with or without a nosegay is a thing we never dream of. Yet let it not be forgotten that no later than yesterday, an old woman—" old Esther of Carstamin,"[4] the likest thing to a

---

[4] Cf. *Reminiscences*, ed. Froude, ii., pp. 156-159; ed. Norton, i., pp. 87-89.

witch that this district has to boast of—presented me with two old plates! I was to keep them "as *a memorandum*"; but so long as she is on foot, I shall not want for a living memorandum. Poor old creature! her father was Laird of Carstamin, and "took lump sugar to his toddy." But the Devil was busy with him—and with Esther too—for she had a child "*by chance*" (she told us), and then two Husbands, *also by chance* it would seem, for one after the other left her so soon as the ready money was spent, and there she sits in a half-roofed hovel on the moor—"a monument of wrath,"—"a widow, yet a wife,"—nay, twice a widow and twice a wife. She totters about people's houses, where she can find them, and picks up scraps either in honesty or dishonesty. If she hear a swine squealing (and her hearing is wonderfully acute in this particular), away she posts in that direction, to try what windfall of tripes or livers may come her way. But, alas! alas! they killed four swine within a gunshot the other day, and "*nane was ever at the pains to say—Hae, Esther, there's a puddin te'e."*[5] Mercy, how I have *clattered* thro' four pages!

What are they thinking in Edinburgh about Mrs. M——? We are deeply interested in Henry, and he has not written *since she was found.* God grant he may not get into any duel. The newspapers throw no light on the business.

I was at Templand last week. My Mother was surprisingly well, considering how she has been harassed of late. My Grandfather was peaceable, tho' still lying in bed. A Mr. Gibson was there.

Sam is requested to settle a small account for Carlyle, and to give you the balance. Get me a pair of *very strong* shoes from Rutherford: he has my measure. There is no hurry about them—only leave them, or, more properly speaking, have the goodness to cause them to be left with Sam, who, with his accustomed helpfulness, will forward them to me. I was sorry to

---

[5] *I.e.* " tae ye "=to you, for you.

hear of his cold; but as he made no mention of it in his note, I trust he is quite recovered. My kindest remembrances to your Uncle. Carlyle joins me in wishing you both very many happy years.

And believe me, ever your affectionate friend till death,

JANE WELSH CARLYLE.

XXX.

To Miss Stodart, 22 George Square, Edinburgh.

["Speed" in corner, but Carlyle has added, "Need not be forwarded."]

CRAIGENPUTTOCH,

Some time in April [Postmark, *April 20th*, 1831].

MY DEAREST ELIZA,—

My first determination, after reading your letter and tasting your barley-sugar, was to write the very next week along with a manuscript for Cochrane.[1] But the manuscript for Cochrane did *not* go the next week, nor the next again, nor is it gone at this hour, but rather doubts are rising in men's minds whether it is ever to go at all. In which circumstances, "necessity, mother of invention," has put me on the discovery that there is *no* indissoluble con-

---

[1] Cochrane was editor of the *Foreign Quarterly Review.*

nection between the said manuscript and the said letter; and this fact being once clearly demonstrated to my understanding, I lose not another moment in courteously saluting you—as in duty and affection bound—" Get ye good morning, Audrey!"[2] and a fine sunshiny spring morning it is. Our woods have put on their green again, and blackbirds are sweetly singing, and hens profitably cackling, and the Bubbly[3] goggeling neither sweetly nor profitably; and, in short, even here one feels oneself still in the land of the living [and] in the place of hope.

My Cousin! did you ever watch a goose hatching, or a turkey, or any hatching thing? If not, you can form no adequate conception of the hopes and fears which at present agitate my breast. I have a goose sitting on five eggs—a rather flighty sort of character—quite *a goose of the world* in fact, who from time to time drives

---

[2] Cf. p. 68, *note* 2, on Letter X.
[3] "Bubbly-Jock" is a Scotch term for the turkey-cock.

me to the brink of despair by following her pleasures whole hours with the other geese to the manifest danger of cooling her eggs. I hover about the nest during these long absences with a solicitude quite indescribable, and it will end, I believe, in my sitting down on the eggs myself. My turkey again sits like a very vegetable (indeed, she could not well do otherwise, being secured under an inverted crate); but she is a born idiot, and I dread that the offspring will be all creatures of weak intellect also—nay, more—that one by one they will be overlaid or otherwise "die from neglect" like Robert's little daughter. "The troubles that afflict the just," etc., etc.! "*Now this comes of having the world!*" as Carlyle's Grandmother said, when by some miracle she found herself in possession of an entire gold guinea, and was at her wits' end where on all the earth to secure it from thieves.[4] When I had no stock, I was comparatively tranquil.

---

[4] Cf. *Letters and Memorials*, i., p. 161, *note*.

> "Angels and ministers of grace defend us.
> Art thou a Spirit of health or goblin damned?"[5]

O Eliza, Eliza! We were sitting at breakfast yesterday morning, expecting nor evil nor good,—sipping a highly nutritive beverage of tea and whipt egg, and talking pleasantly enough on some transcendental subject, when suddenly—an unusual sound of carriage wheels, louder and louder, nearer and nearer, interrupted the whole operation. I thought it could be no one else but Miss Anderson, of Sanquhar, and ran to receive her "in my choicest mood!"[6] But, Lord have mercy! what was I come out for to see? Seated in an open gig, muffled curiously in Indian shawls, my astonished eyes rested on the large muscular figure of—Miss ——! Yes, Mary ——, of Haddington. "*Hee, hee, hee! Mrs. Caarlile! Hee, hee, hee!*" But it was no hee-heeing to me! The intensity of my astonishment quite

---

[5] "Angels and ministers of grace defend us!
Be thou a spirit of health or goblin damned," etc.
Hamlet, Act. i., Sc. 4.

[6] Cf. p. 145, *note* 2 on Letter XXIII.

paralyzed me, and it was minutes before I could express the joy which I really always feel at recognising a Haddington face, belong to whom it may. She was obliged to be off the same evening. But we made the best use of our time. I took nothing in hand the whole day but *milking* news from her (a rather rural metaphor), which she with unabating copiousness supplied; and could I tell you but a tenth of the facts wherewith I in this way stored my mind, you would wonder equally at the capacity of the Instructor and the Learner. Nothing, I think, in her whole budget amused me so much as *a Tale of a nettle*—a still more serious nettle-feud than the "*Jenny Nettles*"[7] of ancient times. Mary Davidson one day stuck a fine fresh little nettle in the back part of Dr. Fyffe's hat, while he was paying a professional visit. The Dr. clapped

---

[7] The precise allusion I cannot explain. According to Jamieson's *Scottish Dictionary*, "jenny-nettle" is a Lanarkshire term for the "daddy-long-legs," called also "jenny-spinner." "The prettiest little Jenny Spinner," says Carlyle, picturing to himself Jane Welsh in her childhood (*Reminiscences*, ed. Froude, ii., p. 98; ed. Norton, i., p. 75).

on the hat without noticing the emblem, walked thro' the whole town with it, and finally mounted and rode off thro' the country. But he detected it at last—the hateful, ridiculous, too appropriate nettle—and then what were his feelings, his boiling rage! "Indignation (they say) makes verses."[8] Accordingly, the Dr. indited "one of the most impertinent," and, I will be bound to say, unintelligible poems ever penned, against the fair offender, whom he styled "*a flirting fool,*" and sent it to the house instead of his further medical attendance. Here is a Doctor for you of a right independent spirit!

Do you know anything of our Mother? She is gone out of sight, for two weeks at least out of my sight; and if I do not hear tell of her soon, I must be *after* advertising her.

Carlyle was for writing a letter to your Uncle *on his own bottom*, but I advised him to add a postscript here by way of saving postage, and

---

[8] "Si natura negat, facit indignatio versum."
Juvenal, *Sat.* i., 79.

now "from thee, Eliza, I must go," being constrained by what is called the iron law of necessity, to take steps (as many as are between here and the next farm *town*) towards getting the above written sent off.

God bless you!

Ever affectionately yours,

JANE BAILLIE PEN[9] WELSH CARLYLE.

To Mr. Bradfute.

MY DEAR SIR,—

Your present of the Cigar Box was no less well-timed than kind; it came on me when my former stock were within a dozen of the end, like a gift of Providence, as well as friend's gift. Many thanks for it! I have tasted the Narcotic, and find it of the right sort; thus, not once, but many times, will I thank you, and if not *drink*, yet heartily *smoke* your health. You who are no smoker cannot understand the force of this. But will you not come hither this Summer and see

---

[9] Cf. p. 111, *note* 6 on Letter XV.

the House of the Wilderness, and the strange wild-people (towards you very tame and loving) that dwell therein? I think you might easily drive a worse road. I could promise you (and your Eliza) a quiet sheltered lodging in a country *new* at least; and the warmest welcome from friends that are not so new.

Believe me always,
My dear Sir,
Faithfully your's,
THOMAS CARLYLE.

[Postscript added by Mrs. Carlyle.]

Aye! will you not come? and eat home-grown strawberries on my Birthday?[10] I know not when I shall see you unless you come hither. My kind regards and C.'s to Sam. The Barley sugar was a precious goody.[11] I had not tasted a morsel for three years.

---

[10] July 14th.
[11] *I.e.* sweetmeat.

SEALS USED BY CARLYLE AND HIS WIFE.

(Double the Size of the Originals.)

7

Carlyle sketched the emblem of the wasting candle, with the motto written on it, '*Terar dum prosim*,' 'May I be wasted, so that I am of use.'"—Froude, *Thomas Carlyle*, A. I., p. 197.

8

Carlyle, writing to his brother Alexander, from London, in January 1825, says: "I have purchased me a small seal and the Carlyles' crest with *Humilitate* and all the rest of it engraven on it."—Norton, *Early Letters of T. Carlyle*, II., p. 300.

9

This must be a copy of the seal sent to Goethe, in 1831, by fifteen English admirers— "The serpent of eternity encircling a star." The motto is taken from Goethe's verses—

> "*Wie das Gestirn*
> *Ohne Hast*
> *Aber ohne Rast,*
> *Drehe sich jeder*
> *Um die eigne Last*"—

which Carlyle roughly renders—

> "Like as a star
> That maketh not haste,
> That taketh not rest,
> Be each one fulfilling
> His god-given Hest"—

in the Essay on "Goethe's Works" in his *Miscellanies*, *Works*, Library Edition, IX., p. 161. See also Norton, *Letters of T. Carlyle* (Second Series), I., p. 285; and Lewes, *Life of Goethe*, p. 559.

XXXI.

To Samuel Aitken, Esqr., Messrs. Bell and Bradfute's, Bank Street, Edin^r.

CRAIGENPUTTOCH,

28*th June,* 1831.

MY DEAR SIR,—

I learn with very great satisfaction that our Friend of Minto[1] has come home so much stronger and heartier; and hope the improvement will continue with him and increase.

To you also I am obliged for letting me know about his Candidateship: I need not say that no such important enterprise on his part can be indifferent to me, that no little service I could conscientiously render him, here or elsewhere, should be wanting. It will always be a most

---

[1] The Rev. David Aitken thought of becoming a candidate for the chair of Church History in Edinburgh University, which had fallen vacant in this year. The town council of Edinburgh were the patrons, but in those days of unreformed corporations were very much under Government influence. I cannot otherwise explain Carlyle's reference to Crown preferments.

pleasant duty to bear testimony of all that I know concerning him (wherein is much good), whensoever or wheresoever I am called upon.

I must warn you, however, that, as matters stand, my writing specially to the Lord Advocate[2] can hardly do much good. In the first place, I myself am very ignorant of Church History, and of who would be a good Professor of it; secondly, I do *not* know whether our Friend is the best that will present himself, but only that I believe him better than most Scotch Clergymen; thirdly, I should fondly trust that with a *Russel-Purge*[3] Administration, Crown preferments will be distributed on public views only, the old Dundas System[4] having become noisome in the nostrils of

---

[2] Francis Jeffrey.

[3] Lord John Russell brought in the Reform Bill on March 1st, 1831, which would have disfranchised sixty " rotten boroughs " and abolished 168 borough seats; so that he is here compared to Colonel Pride " purging " the House of Commons in 1648.

[4] Henry Dundas, first Viscount Melville (1742-1811), was practically the ruler of Scotland under Pitt. For an account of the " Dundas System," from the Whig point of view, see Cockburn's *Life of Jeffrey*, p. 74 (ed. 1872); it

all men; so that the circumstance of Mr. Aitken's *being my Friend,* tho' never so emphatically stated, could have no weight here.

On these grounds, more especially as the matter cannot be decided for a good while, I think it will be better at all events to wait. If, in the course matters take, I see any prospect of doing Mr. A. an honest service (which will be doing Justice herself one), then depend upon it no one will *more zealously* endeavour. Will you, as anything decisive occurs of a promising sort, be so good as let me know: a Letter (perhaps an old Newspaper), always welcome, will show me how it stands. It is not impossible that I may be in London[5] before the thing is settled and *see* the Lord Advocate.

---

should be remembered that Cockburn was allied through his family to the Dundases. In his *Memorials* he says: "Within this pandemonium [the old council chamber] sat the town council, omnipotent, corrupt, impenetrable. Nothing was beyond its grasp; no variety of opinion disturbed its unanimity, for the pleasure of Dundas was the sole rule for every one of them" (p. 83, ed. 1872).

[5] Carlyle went up to London in August. See Froude, *Thomas Carlyle,* A. ii., p. 163 ff.

We are well here; and send our best regards to George Sq :

Many thanks for your punctuality in all Business matters.—In great haste with both a Wife and Maidservant calling on me to Tea,

  I remain,
    My Dear Sir,
      Faithfully your's,
        THOMAS CARLYLE.

XXXII.

To Miss Stodart, 22 George Square, Edinburgh.

CRAIGENPUTTOCH,
Somewhere about the beginning of October.
[Postmark, *Oct.* 10*th*, 1832.]

MY DEAREST ELIZA,—

"It is surprising to see all how they *ack*' i' the various places," as Mr. Jeffrey's maid, who now, poor creature, acts no longer on this planet, used to preface her travels' history on the dicky of her Master's chaise—an ominous beginning, which, like our Mother's, "O, I must tell you about Aberdeen!" had always the effect of instantaneously scattering her fellow-servants to the four winds as if a bombshell had been thrown into the midst of them. It is really surprising how they ack', not knowing but the next hour may be their last—certain that a *last* must come *soon*, yet leaving the most palpable duties undone as if there were all eternity to do them in. You may guess I am incited to this highly novel and striking reflection by the consideration that my last letter to you has been left unanswered for one year and [a] half, that from anything I hear you are not even *remotely* purposing to answer it—have not a single compunctious visiting[1] about the matter. Yet how many years and half, think you, even at the longest allowance, shall we remain sojourners together on the same earth? and how will the survivor like to remember periods of silence like this, when the possibility of friendly intercourse, then for the first time, like all things *past*, not only rightly estimated, but over-estimated, will exist no more for ever? Nor in censuring you do I pretend altogether to clear myself. I should have written again and again; not only Scripture, which bids you turn the other cheek when one is smitten, but my

---

[1] "That no compunctious visitings of nature
    Shake my fell purpose."
    Macbeth, Act i., Sc. 5.

own experience of how naturally one may fall into a fault from which it is extremely difficult to get out, as well as kindness, which is continually reminding me that you are my earliest friend—all counselled this, but pride and indolence carried the day. In prolonged bad health and worse spirits, I judged there could be small call upon [me] to be sending letters out, as it were, into infinite space, no sounds of them ever more heard. Still vainer seemed it to apply for sympathy to one who was apparently nowise concerning herself whether I remained behind in a nice, flower-potted London churchyard, or returned in a state of total wreck to my own country. A few days before I left London a certain Dr. Allan said to Carlyle in a complimentary tone, as I left the room, "Mrs. Carlyle has the remains of a fine woman."[2] Think of that now! at thirty to pass

---

[2] Mrs. Carlyle was in London with her husband during all the winter of 1831-32. See Froude, *Thomas Carlyle*, A. ii., pp. 203 ff. "There's the remains of a fine woman about

for a remains! Judge if I must not have suffered somewhat, and if loss of health and loss of looks were not a decent sort of excuse at least for not enacting the amiable part of turning the second cheek, or in other words writing the second letter. The short and the long of the matter is, we are both in fault; let us mutually forgive, kiss and be friends, and draw this practical inference that indolence, as the copy line says, is truly the root of all evil.[3]

The special object of my breaking silence this day is to give you a commission which I think will gratify you, not of the petty needle and stay-lace sort, but what think you? To look about in your walks between this and the beginning of winter for a little furnished house to contain my Husband, self, and a maid for as many months as we see good to exchange our

---

Sairah," says Mr. Bailey junior, in *Martin Chuzzlewit*, of Mrs. Gamp.

[3] Seems to be "Satan finds some mischief still," etc., paraphrased on the analogy of "The love of money is the root of all evil."

country life for your town one. The grim prospect of another winter in this solitude is too frightful for my Husband, who finds that it is absolutely essential for carrying on, not only his craft, but his existence, to hear from time to time a little human speech.[4] Accordingly, we are to neighbour you this winter, and let us see to make better of it than on [a][5] former occasion. As to the manner of house, I may begin by restricting your quest by three limitations: first, it must be free of bugs; secondly, of *extraordinary* noises; and lastly, of a high rent; such a place as that my Mother tenanted of Miss Sheriff would answer well enough; perhaps Miss Dora, if it were modestly suggested to her, might make another migration into the country. She never seemed to s[t]ay

---

[4] "I must to Edinburgh in winter; the solitude here, generally very irksome, is threatening to get injurious, to get intolerable."—Carlyle in his journal of September (?) 1832 (Froude, *Thomas Carlyle*, A. ii., p. 310).

[5] Perhaps "the" was the word she meant to put. It will be observed that several words have been omitted in this letter, showing weariness in the writer.

at home on any account but because she had a
house on [her] hands. Henry Inglis represented
Comely Bank as being inhabited now by strange,
haggard, ruffian-looking people, whose calling
was questionable. In that case it were no
longer pleasant, but otherwise I should still
prefer it to any part of the new town; a floor
in the heart of the town were my last resource; any *suburban* situation—especially if
self-contained, were preferable; the nearer yourself the better, and [6] . . . With respect to
house-room, there would be required, at least,
a sitting room and bedroom, with some sort of
adjunct that might be slept in "at a time";
a kitchen, and six feet for the maid; a small
patch outdoors accommodation were extremely
desirable, where my husband might smoke. It
was most piteous to see him reduced to perform
that process in London on the top of a cistern!
looking, as he stood perched aloft "on that bad

---

[6] Some words have been deleted here, and "Second
thoughts are best" is written under them.

eminence,"[7] with the long pipe in his mouth, for all the world like the emblem over a tabacconist's door. Now look round you and see what is to be had, and on what terms, and report progress; and, as the time draws on and my knowledge increases, I will give you more definite instructions.

Does your Uncle ever make the *smallest* mention of me? ever inquire if the mischievous creature who broke his folder[8] is still working devilry on this planet? Alas, no! she is sober enough now—a long succession of bad days

---

[7] " High on a throne of royal state, which far
    Outshone the wealth of Ormus and of Ind,
    Or where the gorgeous East with richest hand
    Showers on her kings barbaric pearl and gold,
    Satan exalted sat, by merit raised
    To that bad eminence."
                    Milton, *Paradise Lost*, ii. 1–6.

[8] Mr. Bradfute used always to employ a folding paper-knife. This I learn from my mother, Eliza Stodart's niece, who has frequently told me of one memorable occasion when Jane Welsh was on a visit to Eliza Stodart at Mr. Bradfute's. The two girls, after saying "Good-night," went, as they often did, to "Uncle Bradie's" bedroom, where a fire was burning, to "do up" their hair and chat before themselves going to

and sleepless nights have effectually tamed her. O Bess, for one good laugh with you, for the sake of old times! I do not remember the time when I laughed. Crying is now the order of the day. Cholera is raging in Dumfries, and the whole town and county in a state of distraction—as if death were now presented to them for [the] first time, because it is presented in a new shape! As if God had not appointed to all men once to die!⁹

---

bed. They had placed his looking-glass on the hearth-rug, and were sitting very comfortably by it, when suddenly they heard the old gentleman coming upstairs rather earlier than usual. Hastily getting up and rushing out, they upset the mirror, and it was broken. Next morning they met him at breakfast time, trembling. But he only remarked, "The *glass* was very *low*, last night, my dears," and was content to take his revenge in a pun.

⁹ Cf. Carlyle's journal of November, 1831, quoted by Mr. Froude (*Thomas Carlyle*, A. ii., p. 226). "All the world is in apprehension about the cholera pestilence, which, indeed, seems advancing towards us with a frightful, slow, unswerving constancy. For myself I cannot say that it costs me great suffering; we are all appointed once to die. Death is the grand sum total of it all." Again in the entry of July 22nd, 1832, when the disease was approaching Dumfriesshire, he writes: "The cowardice or bravery of the world mani-

A kiss to your Uncle, kind regards to Sam. What is Mr. Simpson doing? Your cousins? everybody? For God['s] sake write to me soon. My Mother is bilious and terrified; my Grandfather as usual. I am going over to-morrow to rouse her.

God bless you!

I am always your affectionate friend,

JANE W. CARLYLE.

---

fests itself best in such a season. Nothing lies in *cholera*, with all its collapses, spasms, blueness of skin, and what else you like, except *death*, which may lie equally in a common catarrh—in the wheel of the nearest hackney coach. Yet here death is original; the dunce, who, blinded by custom, has looked at it in the usual forms, heedless, unreasoning, now *sees* it for the first time, and shudders at it as a novelty" (*ib.*, p. 285). In a footnote on the same page is a reference to the severity of the pestilence in Dumfries. Cf. Norton, *Letters of Thomas Carlyle* [Second Series], ii., p. 69, *note* 2. Mrs. Carlyle writes to Carlyle's mother [in 1833?] about cholera: "The answer to all such terrors is simply what Carlyle said a year ago to some one who told him in London: 'Cholera is here': 'When is death not here?'" (Froude, *Thomas Carlyle*, A. ii., p. 351.)

XXXIII.

To Miss Stodart, 22 George Square.

CRAIGENPUTTOCH,
Monday [Oct. or Nov.? 1832].[1]

MY DEAREST ELIZA,—

I was in the hurry of packing and preparing for a little journey, when Carlyle told me he was sending a parcel to Sam, if I had anything to add. To be sure I had several things, but found myself obliged to wait a more convenient season. I have been on my travels ever since, first to Templand, thence to Scotsbrig, back to Templand again, and home the night before last; and now before setting out again I take advantage of this short breathing space to acknowledge your favour and despatch a windfall of pheasants that is come in my way, one

---

[1] The pheasants and the reference to Martinmas (p. 208), taken together, fix this letter after Oct. 1st, and some time before Nov. 11th (or, rather, 22nd—the "old" term-day).

of which have the kindness to give to Sam with my love. I must be back to Templand this week; for my Mother is ailing, and, tho' Isabella Macturk is there, I am not at all easy in leaving her. Her ailment is singular enough. She has no sickness, no pain, looks as well as ever she did in her life, takes her food as usual, only from time to time, perhaps twice or thrice in the course of the day (always when she "sits up for any length of time"), a "feeling of sinking" comes over her, which, tho' it lasts but a few minutes, and never goes the length of complete fainting away, terrifies her to such a degree that she lies almost constantly in bed. Dr. Russel[1] calls it nervous debility, and seems to have no serious apprehension about it. I have a theory of my own about it, and tho' not positively alarmed am anxious and uneasy. Indeed, I am harassed on all sides at present; for, when there, I fancy everything going to wreck at home, the maid to whom I am obliged to commit my Husband and house, cow, hens, etc., etc., being a creature without sense or principle, whose depredations are only to be checked by help of blacksmith's fingers.

I liked your description of Miss Fraser's house, and am inclined to think it would suit very well; the *quantity* of accommodation is suitable, the rent is suitable, and so far as I recollect the situation is suitable. I should *prefer* an *upper* flat, provided there was nothing above. But your plan is good, to ascertain what is to be had, and then for me to see and fix with my own eyes; no, see with my own eyes and fix with my own volition (the schoolmaster of Southwick asked an Irishman if he could read : " Yes, your honour, some little ; but not so well as you, thank God"). The only thing is my weak nervous state of body, which makes me boggle at anything like active exertion; indeed, I never go a journey from home without being worse for days after; but I may be stronger when the time comes—about three weeks or so after Martinmas, we calculate.

And now, having said the needful, I shall not strive with this worst of pens any longer, having to write to my Mother, and make a cheese before bedtime. There will be time in the long winter nights to turn one's whole interior inside out. My kindest love to your Uncle. God bless you, Dear.

Your affectionate

JANE W. CARLYLE.

XXXIV.

[Mrs. Welsh's father, Walter Welsh, died in the latter part of November, 1832. See Froude, *Thomas Carlyle*, A. ii., pp. 316, 317.]

To Miss Stodart, 22 George Square, Edinburgh.

CRAIGENPUTTOCH,

Tuesday Night [Postmark, *Dec. 5th*, 1832].

MY DEAR ELIZA,—

We returned from Templand last week, our presence there being no longer needful, but rather disconvenient, every bed being occupied with new comers, and the sofa to boot. Want of consideration in the male half of the creation is no novelty, so one need not wonder at these individual men; but it is a pity that my mother should have her hands full of *that* sort of occupation, when it were so much better for her that she were folding them to sleep. Mercifully there has been no return of her nervous disorder, but she is bilious and weak, and likely to be worse, when the excitement from so many causes ceases to act on her. My uncle and Alick spoke of leaving a day or two ago. Walter and a Mr. G—— from Glasgow (a recent acquaintance whom I saw on this occasion for the first time with small emotion of thankfulness) were expected to go sooner; but, as neither my Mother nor Isabella McTurk (who also is still there) wrote on Wednesday according to promise, to tell us when we should return, I conclude them to be all still there: and till I hear to the contrary, shall mind my affairs at home, which a three weeks' absence and a change of servants in the interim had brought into extreme disorder. The Edinburgh project has of course been lying quite dormant in the midst of all this distress and serious business. It is only within the last two days we are returned to the consideration of it. Carlyle thinks we should remove about the time when the Christmas dinners are eaten and done. Will you write and tell me what success has attended your house-hunting?—whether Miss Fraser's be still vacant? how soon we could enter after fixing? As my experience of furnished houses is very slight, it would also throw considerable light on my packing operations if you would give me a sort of abridged history of the goods and chattels! (not of each individual house, but the likeliest among them.) For instance, should I need to bring bed and table-linen, spoons, etc.? Have you remarked any pressing dearth in the crockery line? Knives and forks, tablecovers, and suchlike items were easily transported. Is there anything on the mantlepieces? That is a leading question—silly as it may look; for the answer will give me a sort of notion of the character of the whole apartment. I have often seen meagre, cold-looking places that a warm table-cover, a box or two, a few trifles tastefully arranged could in a few seconds, at almost no cost, make plenished and home-looking.

Would to Heaven the little flitting were well over: *"at my time of life and with my cough, going up to Jerusalem* "[1] is an enterprise of weight and danger.

My Mother will surely come to us in the course of the winter, and resume her old connexions. I have not made the proposal yet; one I *did* make —to come hither for a week or two—being violently waved[2] aside, in a way which showed me she should have leisure left her to collect herself before any proposed change would meet a favourable hearing. Her plans are unknown to me, and I believe uncertain to herself. It seems likely she will give up the farm, retaining the house, the garden, and a park;[3] for she has *gained* nothing by the farming hitherto except annoyance.

---

[1] "Going up to Jerusalem," may be taken from Carlyle's father. Carlyle, writing to his brother Alexander, in 1827, says, "Though I should go to Jerusalem seeking health, and die by the road" (Norton, *Letters of Thomas Carlyle* [Second Series], i., p. 68). Prof. Norton refers to *Reminiscences*, i., p. 49 (i., p. 62, in ed. Froude), where Carlyle's father says, "I will rather go to Jerusalem, seeking farms, and die without finding one."

[2] *Sic. Qu.* waived?

[3] "A park" in Scotland means simply an enclosed field, a paddock.

A house of her own she should always have somewhere, however little she may occupy it, and as well there as elsewhere. We live here very comfortably, keeping one maid, a boy, two horses, and a cow on considerably less money than her yearly income; and Templand is a cheaper place for living than this, being nearer all necessary things. But my Uncle will probably get some arrangement set on foot before he leaves. Her present affliction is likely to be severely felt, and just for the very reason that will make it seem to others comparatively light, the long period of confinement, fatigue, and anxiety by which it was preceded. She now feels that dreariest of all feelings—that her occupation is gone, that her last evident duty in the world *has been fulfilled.* But, so long as one lives, new duties show themselves, and by-and-by she will find something to exercise her unwearied activity and feelings of kindness. In the meantime God help her and all of us.

You received a letter from me with the books, in which I expressed my predilection for Miss

Fraser's house?[4] If not, you will hardly see the propriety of the present. God bless you, dear! My love to Bradie, in which my Husband joins.

Your affectionate

JANE W. WELSH.[5]

---

[4] See preceding Letter, pp. 206, 208.
[5] *Sic.* Apparently she was going to write "Jane W. Carlyle," but wrote "Welsh" instead of Carlyle.

XXXV.

To Miss Stodart, 22 George Square, Edinburgh.

Templand,
Thursday [Postmark, *Dec.* 21*st*, 1832].

My dear Eliza,—

Owing to the singularity of our relation with the Post office, as with all the other institutions of active life, your letter only reached me last night, nearly a whole week after date. I am certainly greatly indebted by the trouble you have, and are so readily taking about us; and have also reason to commend the punctuality and distinctness of your communications. It is a grand, and, I am sorry to say, a rare quality in a female letter to carry its meaning on its face; so much so, indeed, that one thinks oneself fortunate to find any meaning at all, after the most puzzling study. But you tell a plain story always, from which one is at no loss to deduce a plain conclusion; and this, however meanly you esteem yourself as a correspondent, makes you to me always an agreeable one.

They say a weak person generally gives *three* reasons where one is all that is required. Accordingly I have three reasons for being sorry we have missed the Grame Street[1] house. I think the climate there healthier than in the New Town; I was pleased with the prospect of being so near to George Square; and finally, I have of late weeks been living there in idea, and got used to the place, as if I had been there in the body. However delays are dangerous, and now there is nothing to be done but to thank our stars that so feasible a looking substitute is cast up, and to put off no time in securing *it*. I think, in all but situation, the Widow's house seems most suitable, and *if you can get it at the rent you speak of*, £4, I beg you will come to a final arrangement with her without delay. I cannot at this moment fix a *day* for entering, but you

---

[1] Grahame Street, Lauriston, must be meant. It is not far from George Square.

may say some day of the first week after New Year's day. Nothing better could be accomplished by my coming in beforehand; and really the notion of going ten miles, without my Husband, is frightful to me, I am so very *feckless*[2] grown. The best plan is for you, as I have said, to take this tenement—and—take possession! the day we are to come, with my old Betty,[3] if you know where to find her, or any other *honest* woman that could put on a fire, and have a kettle boiling on it. I mean to bring a little black maid along with me, who will sort[4] the beds for us in no time; and next day, when we have all our luggage out of the way, we will willingly go home with you to dine with Bradie, if he be willing. You would need to order in a temporary supply of coals, and leave all the rest to my forecasting spirit. The Lady, if she know her own interest, should not hesitate to

---

[2] *I.e.* helpless.

[3] See p. 27, Letter V., *note* 10.

[4] *I.e.* arrange, make tidy, make ready. Is it necessary to explain that "black" does *not* imply "negro"?

let her house to *such* tenants, even at a reduced rent, for I am sure more careful people, more free of children and nuisances of all sorts, are not easy to be fallen in with.

I came hither last Sunday, and found my Mother alone, and not worse than when I left her. But she is still delicate, and suffering exceedingly from the cold weather. I think she will come to us before long, but the *air* of Stockbridge [5] will be a new objection. She hopes to hear from you soon, and sends her kind love, as also does my Husband. We go home on

---

[5] A part of Edinburgh lying in the valley of the Water of Leith. Carlyle gives a pleasing description of this house (18 Carlton Street) in a letter of January 8th, 1833, to his brother John (Norton, *Letters* [Second Series], ii., p. 74): "You remember Stockbridge, and a smart street, with large trees growing through the pavement, looking into the river (Water of Leith), called *Dean Street*? You just cross the Bridge, from Edinburgh, and Dean Street stretches to the *left*. Now Carlton Street is the first street at right angles to that: our house is the corner one (the corner *farthest* from the River), and fronts two ways; both beautiful, one of them into a sort of circus or double-crescent [St. Bernard's Crescent], where are such trees that a rookery has established itself in them."

Saturday to commence a household earthquake. If you cannot read this, blame my mother's infamous pens. A kiss to Bradie. God bless you both.

Ever your affectionate
JANE.

XXXVI.

To Miss Stodart, 22. George Square, Edin^r.

TEMPLAND, THORNHILL,
22nd Decr., 1832.

MY DEAR MISS STODART,—

Jane wrote you a very long letter; but I find on inquiry that two of the most important items are forgotten. My Brother told her long ago that Forgetfulness was stealing over her; that a general "breaking up of the faculties" had become visible.

The two things forgotten are: first, that at Craigenputtoch we have only *one post day in the week;* the day that corresponds to your Tuesday afternoon: a Letter sent from you (I think, before 5 o'clock) reaches us next night in that way; if missed then, it must lie, in all human probability, for another week. Let this therefore be a word to the wise. The second thing I had to remind you of, "dearly beloved," as we of the Pulpit say, is that you must in no wise forget to give us the precise address of the House in your *next* letter; so that we may be able to write carrier directions, post-office directions, and so forth, without loss of time.

If anything *else* is forgotten, do you by natural sagacity find it out and accomplish it! Could you want any wider commission?

We are here till Monday; Mrs. Welsh appeared too weak to-day for leaving. She will not consent to accompany us to Edin^r., but I think will join us there. What new arrangements are to be made at Templand does not yet altogether appear: there is time enough for considering.

Now let us find you at your post, well and giving welcome;—and so be a glad meeting appointed for us all!

With kind remembrances to "Uncle," whom we hope to see often,

I remain,
Dear Eliza,
Yours very truly,
THOMAS CARLYLE.

XXXVII.

To Miss Stodart, 22. George Square, Edin^r.

CRAIGENPUTTOCH, DUMFRIES,
26th Dec^r., 1832.

MY DEAR ELIZA,—

Your very punctual and distinct Communication has just come to hand; and the whole *burble*[1] into which the jolly Widow's peculiar quality of brain has thrown you becomes manifest. Jane seems so thunderstruck and overawed in glancing into the profundities of that matter (wherein she can see no bottom), that I, at her most earnest request, have undertaken to reply to you, as Edward Irving says, "with my own hand."[2]

Two words, it may be hoped, after all will bring us fairly thro'. The first word is that we

---

[1] See p. 62, *note* 4 to Letter IX.
[2] One of Irving's "Apostolic" affectations (see Gal. vi. 11, 2 Thess. iii. 17), alluded to also in *Letters and Memorials*; e.g. i. p. 5.

intend to stay some three months, and shall of course need a house for that time. Take No. 18 for us then, if the woman will engage to let it (and not again to change her mind) on the following principle: That if during the first fortnight we give her warning that the place does not suit, we are to pay her the Six Pounds for one month; and that if no such warning is given, the rent is to be Four Pounds per month all the way, or Twelve Pounds for twelve weeks. If she do not like these terms, wish her good morning, and let her find a tenant elsewhere.

The second word is that as Mrs. —— appears to be (I grieve to say) a Lady of very peculiar habits of doing business, it will be needful for *you* to be doubly and trebly accurate, and see with your own eyes that all minor arrangements (such as that of "getting things"—which I do not well understand) be placed on such a footing that even a Goose cannot mistake them. "Folly to Folly," saith the Proverb, "makes nothing but Melancholy." The proper way is Wisdom to Folly.—As to *Beds*, I hear *Missus* say that she can do without feather-beds, if all the rest be right; and that as to the " getting of things," her expectations are by no means high.

Now this is the answer. I grieve very much for all the trouble you are getting; but you are well known as a most friendly being; and to the heart of sensibility that feels for others' woes,[3] all these things are light and but the luxury of doing good.

I add only that if this negociation take effect, you are likely to have the inexpressible pleasure of seeing us, on the evening of Monday (I think, the 7th of January) by the Thornhill coach; and that we shall hope to hear from you, in any case, this day week.

We left Mrs. Welsh tolerably well yesterday

---

[3] " Teach me to feel another's woe," occurs in Pope's *Universal Prayer*, of which Carlyle wrote in 1868: " No prayer, I find, can be more appropriate still to express one's feelings, ideas, and wishes in the highest direction " (Froude, *Thomas Carlyle*, B. ii., p. 371. The passage is quoted by Prof. Masson in his second lecture on *Carlyle*, p. 82). " Luxury of doing good," is Goldsmith's; cf. p. 166, Letter XXVI., *note* 5.

Q

(the day before having proved a tempest), and came hear[*] to eat a Christmas Dinner, which differed in no visible particular from any other of the year.

With kind regards to Mr. Bradfute; and hoping soon to see you and thank you,

I remain,
Dear Eliza,
Always faithfully yours,
T. CARLYLE.

---

[*] *Sic.*

XXXVIII.

To Miss Stodart, 22 *George Square,*

[Early in March,[1] 1833.]

MY BELOVED COUSIN,—

It would have been hard to conjecture how the flight of *Sapio*[2] the Singer to the Abbey[3] could produce any perceptible effect on the

---

[1] Carlyle writes from 4 Great King Street, on March 26th, 1833 (Norton, *Letters,* etc. [Second Series], ii., p. 91), and he and his wife leave in May after " two months " (see foot of next page).

[2] "An Italian vocalist of this name was professor of singing in Paris, and the vocal instructor of the Empress [*sic !*] Maria Antoinette. He emigrated to England during the French Revolution. His son A. SAPIO, b. London, 1792, held a commission in the army for a short time, afterwards became a tenor vocalist, and made his *début* in the 'Messiah' in 1822. He sang also at York and Edinburgh, and sang on the stage from 1824. Appeared at Drury Lane Theatre, London, 1824, and afterwards sang chiefly in opera. Died (?)."—James D. Brown, *Biographical Dictionary of Musicians,* Paisley, 1886. In Oxberry's *Dramatic Biography,* vol. i., p. 252 (London, 1825), is a contemporary account of this, the younger, Sapio, and a portrait of him as "Carlos."

[3] The precincts of Holyrood were a debtors' sanctuary.

destinies of Thomas Carlyle and his amiable and excellent wife! Yet so strangely are things woven and warped together in this world. We who never saw Mr. Sapio with our eyes or heard him with our ears are proved to have had a lively interest in his running in debt, the consequence of which has been his running to the Abbey, and the consequence of his running to the Abbey has been the evacuation of a furnished house belonging to my old schoolfellow Mrs. Blacky, and the consequence of the evacuation of the furnished house has been an offer on the party of Mrs. Blacky of the said house to me at any rent I liked, and the consequence of the offer has been my acceptance of the same; and thus, thro' the intervention of Mr. Sapio, or rather, to go to the root of the matter, of the Devil who tempted Mr. Sapio, we find ourselves on the eve of removing to No. 4 Great King Street, with the blessed prospect of remaining in town two months longer than the appointed time; and what may be the consequence of our remaining so long, no mortal can predict.

Our charming young friend upstairs has been creating such an infernal disturbance of late,[4] that we were resolved, should any resource present itself, to leave her the house to herself. Accordingly, so soon as I had heard of and seen the King Street floor and found that we *could make it do*, I despatched a highly diplomatic note to Mrs. —— stating our grievance and "making no doubt that she would allow our agreement to terminate at the end of the present week!" The Lady called next day; I was out, but Carlyle received her; she was in the most accommodating mood—"we were quite at liberty to leave whenever it suited us." She made no secret of her participation in the matter. "She was quite aware of the night-noises.—had left the house in consequence of having such disagreeable and disreputable neighbours!" So you and I know what to do, dear, when we happen to have a house we can no longer occupy ourselves—just swear it is all

---

[4] Cf. Froude, *Thomas Carlyle*, A. ii., p. 326.

right and tight, and let it to some innocent third party.

No further word from Templand. I wrote again to-day. It is not so much matter now *when* she comes, but no thanks to her for the respite.

We are invited to dine at your cousin John's on Friday. I must send an apology to the Thomsons' to-night. I have been very ill for two days; on Thursday night the pain in my head was so intense that I fainted entirely away under it.

But "it will not be permanent," as Carlyle tells me; as if I could fancy it would be permanent without instantly cutting my throat.

I am sorry to leave this sweet neighbourhood, and nice, well-aired house. But "what could the fellow do, Sir?" Just that night I was so ill, there was a bacchanalian party over me till three in the morning. I wonder if Mr. Sapio has left any bugs behind him? that is my next terror. I went into a sale of furniture the other day, and partly for the fun of hearing myself *bid*, I bade for an easy chair, and to my infinite surprise it was knocked down to me at 17 shillings. For a moment I was pleased with my bargain, when my Aunt Ann asked, " God bless me, Jeanie, what do you want with that; are you sure there are no bugs in it?" A mortal fright came over me, but just then a Lady thought proper to affirm that *she* also had bade 17 shillings for the chair; and, according to the rules of the sale, it must be put up again. Next time I was more prudent, and kept my tongue quiet, and saw the foolish people bid it up to 28 shillings.

Did I leave one of my bracelets at the Square? if not, I lost it on the road home, the more's the pity. Mr. Fletcher was here the other day— very charming. " Mrs. —— from the country," just the old compound of levity and sentimentality. I like Cooper's novels. Jeffrey writes to me that he has seen Harriet Martineau,[5] and

---

[5] For Harriet Martineau's kindlier opinion of Jeffrey, see her *Autobiography*, i., pp. 314-317.

does not like her at all: "firstly, because she is most excessively ugly; and secondly, because there is nobody good enough for her to admire," —not even *himself*, I presume. And now God bless you. Love to your uncle.

Your affectionate
JANE W. CARLYLE.

18, Carlton Street,
   Saturday.

XXXIX.

To Miss Stodart, 22 George Square, Edinburgh.

CRAIGENPUTTOCH,

24*th* May [Postmark 1833].

MY DEAR ELIZA,—

You have been thinking doubtless (for the heart of woman is prone to evil thoughts) that I did not display alacrity enough in writing to you. But judge not without knowledge; first hear the dolorous tale I have to tell, and you will find that my friendship has in this case been without reproach.

You have first to learn that we were in Edinburgh *two days* after you and all our acquaintance supposed us gone! actually *secreted* in Mrs. Blackey's house, with feelings which I should suppose akin to a ghosts—for, O tell it not in Gath, Eliza! we had—missed the coach! The *old* horror had been transacted anew! And well might we keep ourselves

secret! well might we hide our diminished
heads,¹ and shun the cheerful face of a friend!
You know *my* way of being always too early—
perhaps *you do not* know that my Husband
always puts off till the last moment: this, almost
the only, discrepancy in our habits has produced
many little argumentations betwixt us which
on that ill-fated morning I for the *first time*
determined to evade. Accordingly, tho' up
in good time (indeed, I did not close my eyes
the whole night), dressed and breakfasted in
good time, we somehow trifled away *five minutes*
over and above what there was to work on,
and on reaching the starting-place, bag and
baggage, saw our "*convenience*" (as Mrs. Rennie
used modestly to call her carriage) vanishing at
the far end of Princes Street!² Let us drop a
veil over the disgraceful home-march! Enough to

---

¹ "—— at whose sight all the stars
　　Hide their diminished heads."
(In Satan's address to the sun: Milton, *Paradise Lost*, iv. 34.)
² Cf. Carlyle *Reminiscences*, ed. Froude, ii., p. 168; ed.
Norton, i., p. 96; Norton, *Letters of Thomas Carlyle* [Second
Series], ii., p. 96. In a letter of 1815, Carlyle calls a coach

say that I was forthwith deposited in bed with the dreadfullest headache, and remained there most of the time we had to wait; glad my existence was unknown, that so I might be left in quiet. It was now too apparent to me that I had got Influenza, I only hoped that I might brave it out, and keep up till I was landed at *home*. But I could get no further than Templand, after suffering by the way such misery as I shall not soon forget. There I had to keep my bed for a week. My Mother too was laid up with it for three days, so I had the additional vexation of being looked on as a pestilence. On Monday I took the road again, reached the goal of all my wishes, for the time being; again had a bad turn that confined me in bed, and only yesterday felt myself like living, and to-day eat half of a salt-herring to breakfast,

---

a "leathern-conveniency" (in quotation marks).—Norton, *Early Letters*, i., p. 28. "Leathern convenience" is used by Scott in *The Antiquary* (1816), chap. i. "Convenience" was applied to vehicles by Smollett and others before him. Dr. J. A. H. Murray tells me of modern monks, in Hungary, calling a carriage "*opportunitas*."

on the strength of which I write. So *confess* that I have lost no time, but on the contrary am displaying a most satisfactory ardour in the matter. We found the house not merely standing, but in the best order. The woman who had charge of it thro' the winter had kept the damp out, and Nancy had sorted[3] it to a wonder without my superintendence. My cow is at the point of calving; my little horse is in high mettle; my hens are fat and laying; and all have returned from their diverse winter-quarters, making together with ourselves a "*re-union*" of the most idyllic description. So far we have cause to be thankful.

But as there is always some confounded drag on the contentment that is of this world, so a spectacle presented itself on our return enough to have made a passionate person *explode*, but me, who am an example of patience and submission, it only moved to tears. One of the woods (just think of it), the one on your left as

---

[3] Cf. p. 218, Letter XXXV., *note* 4.

you approach the house, was burnt to cinders! A melancholy mass of blackened stumps, while all around was shining in new verdure. The tenant had been burning heather. The trees had caught fire, and he simply retired into his house and left it to burn![4] O Eliza, I could cry yet to think of this—to think of my Father taking such a world of pains to plant these woods—to think they have had rain and sunshine vouchsafed them for more than twenty years, to be finally consumed in one night thro' the carelessness of a lout like Macadam!

---

[4] Cf. Norton, *Letters of Thomas Carlyle* [Second Series], ii., p. 101. "The only thing of any consequence that has gone out of joint is one of the Plantations which M'Adam's people have burnt, in burning their heather. The careless lumber!" See also Carlyle, *Reminiscences*, ed. Froude, ii., p. 157; ed. Norton, i., p. 87: "I remember one frosty kind of forenoon, while walking meditative to the top of our Hill (now a mass of bare or moorclad whinstone *Crag*, once a woody wilderness, with woody mountain in the middle of it, 'Craigen*puttock*,' or the stone-mountain 'Craig' of the 'Puttock,'—puttock being a sort of *Hawk*, both in Galloway Speech, and in Shakespeare's Old English [see *Cymbeline*, Act. i., Sc. i., line 140]; 'Hill-Forest of the Puttocks') now a very bare place," etc.

But he pays his rent, and that is everything: the appearance of Craigenputtoch is of consequence only to *us*. Well, be it so! we shall not stay to see it reduced to its original desolation. I wish its improvement had not been my Father's work, and then I should not care tho' it were let on a nineteen years' lease to the Devil himself. One thing, however, I shall insist on; namely, that I should hereafter have the melancholy privilege of being *informed* when my property is burnt or otherwise destroyed, instead of having the fact concealed from me till it could be concealed no longer—even my own servant commanded by my Mother not to tell me of it. You see I am angry—more so, perhaps, than becomes a pretender to some Philosophy. But I am giving vent to my feelings on the occasion *here* for the first time, as a way of getting in some measure rid of them. To turn to a more agreeable topic. Will you give our affectionate regards to your Uncle, of whose kindness to us during our stay in town, from the first day to the last (a sort of kindness so much after our hearts), my Husband and I have many times gratefully commemorated? Do you too, my dear Eliza, accept our kind remembrances of your kindness. Write to me soon, and love me always.

Your affectionate
JANE W. CARLYLE.

When you see Mrs. John, pray apologize to her in my name for my incivility in going off without seeing her after her manifold civilities towards me. I did not give up the intention of calling, till ten o'clock on Monday night, when I found I had still so much to do that it was impossible; for the whole day had been taken up with callers. During the two subsequent *private* days I was too ill; besides, I could not have made my neighbourhood known to one without offence to my Aunts and you and others.

XL.

To Miss Stodart, 22 George Square, Edinburgh.

CRAIGENPUTTOCH,

28*th July* [Postmark 1833].

DEAREST,—

I salute you with undiminished regard, and sincerely thank you for your letter. It is the only "voice from *Edinburgh*" that has reached us since we left, save a hysterical giggle from John G—— about his marriage. If we were not in closer connexions with London, whence we have news every week, we should remain in total ignorance "how they ack' i' the various places,"[1] and might come in time to be as great curiosities of innocence as the king and queen of the Sandwich Islands, who, poor things! stuffed themselves to death, if you remember: a more touching instance of overeating is nowhere on record.[2]

---

[1] Cf. Letter XXXII., p. 197.
[2] In 1824 the king and queen of the Sandwich Islands

From overeating the association is natural to digesting, so I shall take the present p[a]ragraph to inform you that of late I have been digesting not ill.

If you were at all instrumental in giving me Influenza, you have the satisfaction to think you gave me a good thing; for I am certainly indebted to it for a considerable improvement in my health, which has been better ever since, than at any time for two years previous. It has even seemed as if my beauty would emerge from its premature eclipse; at least it has occasionally struck me that my glass reflected something more than "the *remains* of a fine woman,"[3] the animated presence of an average sort of

---

visited England, and both died in a London hotel of measles —said to be aggravated by change and excess of diet. A correspondent, writing from Aberdeen, tells me she has heard the late Mr. S. C. Hall relate that Theodore Hook made a couplet on the occasion:

"'Waiter, two Sandwiches!' cried Death;
And straight their Majesties resigned their breath."

The same event is alluded to in *Letters and Memorials*, ii., p. 154.

[3] Cf. Letter XXXII., p. 199.

woman. Nothing indeed *that* to found conceit upon; but like *the penny roll* it may be "*made to do*," and better thus perhaps than to be "ower fou hadin,"† as the proverb goes. For instance, had the queen of the Sandwich Islands been but restricted to a penny roll!

On the whole this summer has passed away pleasantly; when I wake in the morning, and wink my eyes, and ascertain that I have still no headache, I spring up in good humour for the day, prepared to take the rest as I find it. The *work* I have done would go little way in furnishing out a set of dining tables (Mrs. Davies's were exhibited to her acquaintance, for three days, before the sale of Ladies' work, spread over with twenty pounds' worth of nick-nacks!); but it is enough to keep my hand in, and the Devil out, who "is always," they say, "at the elbow of an idle man," still more of an idle woman. I am more intent in getting all the good possible from the free access one

---

† "Over full holden," *i.e.* too well off.

has here to the open air. I am out and in all day long; neither walking nor working with any continuance, but combining all sorts of exercise and all sorts of tasks in the most rapid alternation. A well-fitting gown and a rather stylish bonnet have received beginning and finish in this way; also one cap, one collar, and one shift. Nor has my hand forgot its cunning in kneading dough and "*pressing the snowy curd*" (no good sign of curd, by the way, which is the better the yellower it is). Accordingly there is a cheese lying in state for your Uncle, with which I have had much sorrow; once, twice, thrice the mice assaulted it, and so often left the impression of their "*beautiful dents*" (as Captain Robinson at Pitca[i]thly used to say), and Lord Minto was not more beside himself when the rats assaulted the cheek of his last born, than I under these audacious attempts. I *could* have fired a pistol; I did better—baited a trap.

Young Hunt is not come nor coming. He got the length of Edinburgh, where he was kindly entertained by Henry Inglis, as we had arranged for him. But the fatigue of the journey and the separation—his first separation—from his own people increased his nervous ailments to such a degree, that he could resolve on nothing but to go back with all despatch the way he came. We have had my Brother-in-law with us for some six weeks; but he soon leaves to return with Lady Clare[5] to Italy, for two years, so that our movements will not for the present be determined by *his* choice of a settlement. Most probably we shall remain where we are next winter, and go somewhere, perhaps abroad, in the spring or summer.[6] We have had no other visitors except my Mother-in-law, for two weeks; and my Mother, Walter, and Helen, for a fly.[7] My Mother has mounted an equipage of a rather fanciful sort; namely

---

[5] Dr. John Carlyle was travelling physician to the Countess of Clare. Cf. Froude, *Thomas Carlyle*, A. ii., pp. 180, 348.

[6] "We think of France next summer." Letter to Eliza Miles, *ib.*, pp. 351–353.

[7] *I.e.* for a flight, a flying visit.

a cuddy⁸ and cart! which travels at the rate of two miles an hour. The whole apparatus, I confess, looks less useful than absurd.

Do you see anything of my Aunts, of anybody belonging to me? My Mother will have told you all about the Donaldsonian expedition, which I forgot in the list of our visitors.

We sadly miss your Uncle's books, and we sadly miss your Uncle's self and his niece. Give him our kindest love. I shall not forget his goodness to us last winter, which had been as great perhaps on former occasions, but which I was more sensible of last winter that at any other time, from seeing how tiresome a person always ailing becomes to ordinary friends. God bless you, Dear. Write soon—all sorts of news, great and small. Unless you had lived here a while, you can have no idea how passionately one desires to be told something.

[*No Signature.*]

---

⁸ *Cuddy*, the usual word in Scotland for a donkey. It is of Gypsy origin.

XLI.

To Miss Stodart, 22 George Square, Edinburgh.

CRAIGENPUTTOCH,
[Postmark, *Nov.* 9*th*, 1833.]

MY DEAREST ELIZA,—

I was aware of your absence and the captivity in which my letter was likely to remain, but I considered it was in excellent quarters, and gave myself no concern either on its account or my own. In any case it would not have occurred to me to accuse *you* of carelessness, however neglectful you may be about *writing*. I should be a wretch not to entertain a deep sense of your willingness and alacrity whenever there is anything to be *done*, and not to give you credit for such on the ground of past experience, in spite of any incidental appearances that might argue the contrary.

The frame I find quite suitable to its contained —*good* and *plain*, just as I could have wished it; the tea proves an excellent article at the money; for the barley sugar I have to return the children's joyful thanks. You were kind to think of *them*, but you are always mindful. *Nota Bene:* The next time there is *a sixpence* over, you may give it to the poor.

It filled me with astonishment that Taylor should have recollected my name and address, having transacted with him only *once* in my life, and to so very limited an extent. What a pity that such a singular business talent should be employed in frame-making, and so little, apparently, to its possessor's profit, even there! I take your congratulations on the benefit received from my Moffat expedition[1] in good part, tho' nothing in the world could be more misplaced. The expedition was *ennuyante* while it lasted, and injurious in its effects. I am hardly yet so well as before I went thither. However, I am much better now than I was last year at this time, and have a sort of moderate hope that I shall by degrees get quite well, or rather as well as ever I was; for, to say the truth, my whole life has been

---

[1] Cf. Froude, *Thomas Carlyle*, A. ii., p. 364.

a sort of *puddling* as to health. Too much of schooling hadst thou, poor Ophelia!² and perhaps too much of dissipation also, if we credit our friend of Kirknewton, who pronounced my "morals corrupted and my constitution ruined," so far back as the year 1817, by means of *one* Leith Assembly! To a certainty my "*charming naïveté*" was then lost for ever and a day, which was the greater pity, since so little charmingness of any other sort remained behind. So I say myself in sincerity of heart, tho' I should not exactly like that another said it.

And here I must positively digress from my digression, just to observe that I wonder I do not send to you a letter once a week instead of once in the six months. It is so pleasant to talk with you about old times, whether by the fireside or on paper, with the profoundest disregard of all sense or ceremony. But so it is. "Man," as Carlyle was saying last night, "is a mass of contradic-

---

² "Too much of water hast thou, poor Ophelia."
Hamlet, Act. iv., Sc. 7.

tions." What a quantity of wisdom, new and old, falls from his lips in the course of one solar day! Had I but Mr. Taylor's memory to keep hold of it. On the crumbs that fall from *his* table I might positively set up a respectable little bread shop of my own, if I were not too indolent to gather them up into a whole. Just figure me dealing out *cats'-meat* after this sort, and realizing a *name* (*over my door*), (most Authors have no more), and a snug little pin-money to boot! This indeed would be, not "*lighting the candle at both ends*," as we see some improvident couples do, but a notable invention for *burning the candle twice over*. But I am all too rapidly approaching the end of my paper, so must "*cease this funning*"[3] (of the *wershest*[4]), and tell you seriously what I am about, not doubting but both your Uncle and yourself, so long and intimately acquainted with my many amiable qualities, are dying with curiosity on this head at all seasons of the year. Know,

---

[3] "Cease your funning"—the first words of a song in Gay's *Beggar's Opera*, Act ii., Air 37.

[4] *Wersh* = insipid.

then (to give the Devil his due, meaning by the
Devil not you but myself), that I have really
been a tolerably good child for some weeks back.
My time (of which valuable commodity the people
here have perhaps more at their own disposal than
any other individuals on the habitable globe) has
been spent more satisfactorily and profitably than
usual. A great Godsend has befallen my Husband this autumn, in which, as in all his other
Godsends and Devilsends, I heartily participate.
John Hunter (who never saw him) has been
induced to confide to him the keys of the Barjarg
Library[5] (an extensive and valuable collection),
with leave to borrow therefrom at discretion.
You cannot figure what an inestimable benefit it
is, in our situation nearly impracticable on this
side, or what exhalations of gratitude rise from my

---

[5] John Hunter was at this time the minister of the Tron
Church in Edinburgh, and was a younger brother of Mr.
Hunter Arundell of Barjarg, some eight miles from Craigenputtoch. This permission to use the library at Barjarg is
referred to in Froude, *Thomas Carlyle*, A. ii., p. 370; Norton, *Letters of Thomas Carlyle* [Second Series], ii., p. 121.
See also Prof. Norton's *note* in his edition of the *Reminiscences*, i., p. 83.

Husband's soul towards the Minister of the Tron. I verily believe if he were in Edinburgh, he would even go and hear him preach, to show his sense of the kindness. Two gig-boxfulls of excellent books have already been brought over and consumed by one party like reek, while I have selected therefrom *Memoirs of Marie Antoinette* (by Mr. Campan), *Œuvres de Mme Roland* (the very best woman I ever scraped acquaintance with), *Mémoires de M[m]e de Staël*, a clever, spirited, little creature, quite superior to the sentimental de Staël-Holstein that I used to make such work about in my '*wee existence*'; and finally a Life of Cook[e] the Actor,[6] as a warning against drunkenness. I have also put thro' hands at the same time a modicum of useful needlework, with the greatest possible despatch; a little gingham frock for my Brother's daughter that is my name-child—the old cloak, rehabilitation thereof (this article of apparel is establishing its claims to the French epithet *éternel*. Carlyle

---

[6] G. F. Cooke, 1755–1812. The *Dict. of National Biography* refers to an anonymous *Life* of him published in 1813.

bought handkerchiefs in the Palais Royal with that recommendation)—a NIGHT-CAP not of the "*the*" sort, but a *night-cap in ordinary*—and lastly, not finished yet, a pellerine, quite a chef d'œuvre of its kind. It is cut out of some old lavender popelin[e] which you must have seen officiating as a gown, not on one, but several members of our family, something like twenty years ago, the gowns of that period being inadequate to make more than a sleeve in the present. I realized out of it in the beginning of summer a singularly elegant bonnet; and the residue is now combining itself into a pelerine, which, lined with wadding and part of the old (villanously bad) crimson persian[7] of the old cloak, will in the gracefullest manner protect my shoulders thro' the approaching inclemencies of the season. O my dear cousin, what a fine thing is a fine natural taste, especially for the wife of an Author, at a time when the booksellers' trade is so low! But,

---

[7] *Persian* = "a thin, plain silk, much used for linings" (Beck's *Draper's Dictionary*).

alas! I am at the end of my sheet, while yet far from the end of my good works. May the Powers of Friendship bless what we have heard; and with our united affection and good wishes to your Uncle, and the like for yourself,

I remain, your obedient humble servant,

JANE W. CARLYLE.

What a shame! I have not mentioned my Mother, and perhaps you have not heard from herself. I have twice. She professes to be better than usual as to health, but I fear she cannot long be happy in Liverpool. They wish to make their guests entirely so, but thro' miscalculation fail lamentably of the result. Thanks and remember me to Sam. Anything of Mrs. John? I often bethink me in sorrow of what you said, that I once wrote a pretty hand, but it was quite fallen off and indeed nearly illegible. Practice, I believe, is the best means of mending it. Write soon then, that I may write soon again.

XLII.

To Miss Stodart, 22 George Square, Edinburgh.

[Postmark, *Jan.* 10*th*, 1834.]

FALSEST of womankind, canst thou declare
All thy fond plighted vows fleeting as air?

Why in the Devil's name don't you write to me? I have a quantity of things to tell you—things new and strange; but what encouragement have I to communicate a single iota of them, since the fullest letter once committed to the post office for you seems sent out into infinite space, procuring me not even so much as an assurance that it has reached its destination!

No, you shall have no *letter*, till you alter your figure as a correspondent! I merely take the opportunity of a frank to the Advocate[1] (who is an example of constancy to such defaulters as you) to suggest to you that human patience has limits, a truth which you seem to have altogether

---

[1] Jeffrey.

lost sight of; and that I begin to be weary of the treatment I experienced here; and so God bless you, and mend you. Your Uncle would use me better, I wager, if he had ever been in the habit of corresponding with me; "but there is no truth in woman's love."

A kiss to him; to you a vehement remonstrance.

Your affectionate, too placable,

JANE W. CARLYLE.

CRAIGENPUTTOCH,
10th January.

XLIII.

[June 10th, 1834, was the date of settling at 5 Cheyne Row. Cf. Carlyle's letters to his mother and to his brother John in Norton (Second Series), ii., pp. 167–186.]

To J. Bradfute, Esqr., 22 George Square.

5. GREAT CHEYNE ROW, CHELSEA, LONDON.

29th July, 1834.

MY DEAR SIR,—

It is surely the duty of some of us to give special notice at George's Square that Craigenputtoch is desolate, and London sending up the smoke of a new hearth: no doubt, you know it already, but one so well-disposed towards us should know it from ourselves. Nevertheless, my wife, I perceive, is too lazy, so I take the duty in my own hand.

If you remember Battersea Bridge, and Don Saltero's Coffee-house (celebrated in the *Tatler*[1]), with the ancient row of red-brick mansions

---

[1] Number 34.

clad with ivy and jasmine, shaded by high old lime-trees, along the bank of the River, you have Cheyne *Walk*, and are within a cat's-leap of Cheyne *Row* (at right-angles to the *Walk*, and otherwise a miniature copy of it), where in my new workshop, still and clear almost as the Craigenputtoch one, I now write to you. We like our old House extremely; have got it all set in order, out even to the little garden and the vine and walnut-tree; have a servant of the best quality, and shall begin by and by to feel once more at home. We have both fair health too; Jane especially is much better than before: the change, so needful under every point of view, is happily *effected*, turn out how it may.

As for Literature and Book-publishing, the more I look at it hitherto, the more confused it looks. Alas, of quite bottomless confusion! Meanwhile, it would seem, Booksellers can actually print Books now, the Author writing them gratis; which is a great improvement compared with former experiences of mine. Not seeking to decipher farther, what is indeed undecipherable, chaotic, fearful, hateful as a madman's dream, I stand by this so comfortable fact; and am actually busy, at all lawful hours, getting ready a new Book; of which (if I be spared alive some months) I hope to show you a copy, and ask your favourable judgement. It is about the French Revolution (but this is a *secret*), and requires immense preparation. What is to follow after that, will follow.

There is nothing passing here but changes of Ministry and other such daily occurences; of which the less one speaks it is perhaps the more charitable. Poor Coleridge, as you may have seen, died on Friday last:[2] he had been sick and decaying for years; was well waited on, and one may hope prepared to die. Carriages in long files, as I hear, were rushing all round Highgate when the old man lay near to die. Foolish carriages! Not one of them would roll near him (except to splash him with their mud) while he lived; had it not been for

---

[2] Coleridge died July 25th, 1834.

the noble-mindedness of Gilman the Highgate Apothecary, he might have died twenty years ago in a hospital or in a ditch. To complete the Farce-Tragedy, they have only to bury him in Westminster-Abbey.[3]

There is now no other Author here of a better than perfectly commonplace character; too many, one grieves to say, are of a worse, of a dishonest and even palpably blackguard character. "My soul come not into *their* secrets, mine honour be not united to *them*!"[4]

---

[3] With these reflections may well be compared Johnson's words: "To insure a participation of fame with a celebrated poet, many who would perhaps have contributed to starve him when alive, have heaped expensive pageants upon his grave" (Boswell's *Johnson*, Dr. G. B. Hill's edition, i., p. 227); and cf. the other parallels given there in *note* 4, especially Moore's lines on *Sheridan:*

"How proud they can press to the funeral array
   Of him whom they shunned in his sickness and sorrow;
How bailiffs may seize his last blanket to-day,
   Whose pall shall be held up by Nobles to-morrow."

Coleridge however escaped the Abbey, and was buried at Highgate.

[4] "O my soul, come not thou into their secret; unto their assembly, mine honour, be not thou united!" (Gen. xlix. 6.)

We have also seen several "celebrated women" of the literary sort; but felt small longing to see more of them. The world indeed is wide enough for all, and each can and shall wish heartily well to all, and faithfully act accordingly:—meanwhile, if poor Mrs. Featherbrain Irrational All-for-glory and Company are walking in the western quarter, we shall do it all the better by keeping ourselves in the eastern.— But, in fine, there is a fraction of worth and wisdom here in London such as I have found nowhere else: let us use this, enjoy it, and be right thankful for it.

I get hardly any news from Edinburgh, well as I love and shall always love that old stone Town. It is hard, but clear and strong, in spirit as in outward form; built on rocks, looking out upon the everlasting sea. May it flourish, and [5] . . . . . . gain dominion over it!

You, my dear Sir, I am afraid, hardly ever

---

[5] A "fold" of the paper has been lost.

write . . . . Bess drives a most lively pen, and never sent us a Letter that . . . . tell her this (a genuine *fact*), and bid her write whether my lazy . . . . Mrs. Welsh sends us intelligence that you are both as well as . . . . cheerfully enjoying your summer there; and for one day at least I . . . . us in the midst of your flowers. As for me, are not, in these very days, "two cigars" (of your giving) constantly in my coat-pocket, when I go out; how should I forget you?

Will you remember me very kindly to my good Mr. Aitken; for whom I think I shall have a commission again by and by? And so all happiness and peacefulness be with you and those dear to you!

I remain,
My Dear Sir,
Yours very truly,
T. CARLYLE.

XLIV.

To Miss Stodart, 22 *George Square, Edinburgh.*

[This letter must be later than Carlyle's of July 29th, to which there is an allusion at the end of this. Cf. the letters to Carlyle's mother at the beginning of vol. i. of *Letters and Memorials* (Sept. and Nov., 1834).]

OUR WELL-BELOVED FRIEND AND COUSIN,—

Mrs. Montagu,[1] who has made "*the fine arts*" her peculiar study, has a pretty and original way of knitting up a ravelled[2] correspondence. Instead of outraging the already outraged with a lengthened apology, she commences with a lively attack,—"is astonished that you have not written to inquire the reason of her silence," "thinks it strange that you should adopt with her

---

[1] Mrs. Basil Montagu, referred to in *Reminiscences* (ed. Froude, ii., p. 163; ed. Norton, i., p. 92) as a correspondent and friend of Mrs. Carlyle. Carlyle's portrait of her comes in the account of Edward Irving (*ib.*, ed. Froude, i., p. 227; ed. Norton, ii., p. 128).

[2] "Sleep that knits up the ravell'd sleave of care."
Macbeth, Act. ii., Sc. 2.

the formal letter for letter system," "is hurt," "is angry," is everything but what you expected, —namely, ashamed of herself,—and you find yourself suddenly, much to your surprise, transformed into the offending party, and thankful for the kind forgiveness with which she ends. This beats out and out our old simple fashion of making confessions of indolence, etc., etc., or telling lies about excessive occupation, and so forth. But, having let you into the secret, I need not play it off upon you this time, only I let you see what I might do if I liked; and I give you, instead of a useless apology, a useful hint, which you may find your account in against enraged correspondents.

Well! is it not very strange that I am here; sitting in my own hired house by the side of the Thames, as if nothing had happened; with fragments of Haddington, of Comely Bank, of Craigenputtoch interweaved with *cockneycalities* into a very habitable whole? Is it not strange that I should have an everlasting sound in my ears, of men, women, children, omnibuses, carriages, glass coaches, street coaches, waggons, carts, dogcarts, steeple bells, door bells, gentlemen-raps, twopenny post-raps, footmen-showers-of-raps, of the whole devil to pay, as if plague, pestilence, famine, battle, murder, sudden death, and wee Eppie Daidle[3] were broken loose to make

---

[3] In *The Heart of Midlothian*, chap. iv. (near the end), Mrs. Howden says: "There was my daughter's wean, little Eppie Daidle—my oe [*i.e.* grandchild], ye ken, Miss Grizel—had played the truant frae the school, as bairns will do, ye ken, Mr. Butler, . . . and had just cruppen to the gallows-foot to see the hanging, as was natural for a wean." But Scott evidently takes "Eppie Daidle" as a characteristic name for a little girl (*daidle*, used also in the diminutive form *daidlie*, means "pinafore"). Lockhart, in his *Life of Scott*, chap. xi. (ii., p. 476, ed. 1888), says of Scott himself: "He had . . . his hand and his blessing for the head of every little *Eppie Daidle* from Abbotstown or Broomielees." I feel sure, therefore, that Mrs. Carlyle had in her mind a nursery rhyme, of which I have received two versions from correspondents, but, in both cases, with "Doockie" instead of "Eppie."

"Wee Doockie Daidle
Toddles out and in,
Eh, but she's a cuttie,
Makin' sic a din.

Aye sae fou o' mischief,
She cares na what I say,
She makes my very heart loup
Fifty times a day."

me diversion? And where is the stillness, the eternal sameness, of the last six years? Echo answers, at Craigenputtoch! There let them "dwell with Melancholy"[4] and old Nancy Macqueen; for this stirring life is more to my mind, and has besides a beneficial effect on my bowels. Seriously I have almost entirely discontinued drugs, and look twenty per cent. better, every one says, and "what every one says must be true."[5] This being the case, you may infer that I am tolerably content in my new position; indeed, I am more and more persuaded that there

---

The other version gives details as to the din:

> "Wee Duckie Daidle,
> Puddlin' out and in,
> Pitter patter, but and ben,
> Makin' sic a din;
>
> Rattlin' in an iron jug,
> Wi' an iron spoon."
> (*Cætera desunt.*)

[4] Probably she is thinking of the last lines of *Il Penseroso*:

> "These pleasures, Melancholy, give;
> And I with thee will choose to live."

[5] Mrs. Carlyle is, probably, not aware that she is quoting Aristotle: ὃ πᾶσι δοκεῖ, τοῦτ' εἶναι φαμέν (*Eth. Nic.* x. 2 § 4).

is no complete misery in the world that does not emanate from the bowels.

We have got an excellent lodgment, of most antique physiognomy, quite to our humour; all wainscoated, carved, and queer-looking, roomy, substantial, commodious, with closets to satisfy any Bluebeard, a china-closet in particular that would hold our whole worldly substance converted into china! Two weeks ago there was a row of ancient trees in front, but some crazy-headed Cockneys have uprooted them. Behind we have a garden (so called in the language of flattery) in the worst order, but boasting of two vines which produced two bunches of grapes in the season, which "might be eaten," and a walnut-tree from which I have gathered almost sixpence worth of walnuts. This large and comfortable tenement we have, *without bugs*, for some two or three pounds more rent than we paid for the pepper-box at Comely bank. This comes of our noble contempt for fashion, Chelsea being highly unfashionable. The only practical disadvantage in this circumstance is that we are far from most of our acquaintances—a disadvantage which I endeavour to obviate by learning to walk. My success is already considerable. I have several times walked ten miles without being laid up. Besides, we are not wholly isolated. Leigh Hunt lives a few doors off. The celebrated Mrs. Somerville is at Chelsea Hospital,[6] within five minutes' walk, and Mrs. Austin[7]

---

[6] Dr. Somerville, her (second) husband, was then physician to Chelsea Hospital (see *Memoirs of Mary Somerville*, p. 153). Miss Martineau speaks of visiting Mrs. Somerville at Chelsea about this time. "It was delightful to go to tea to her house in Chelsea, and find everything in order and beauty;—the walls hung with her fine drawings; her music in the corner, and her tea-table spread with good things. In the midst of these household elegancies, Dr. Somerville one evening pulled open a series of drawers, to find something he wanted to show me. As he shut one after another, I ventured to ask what those strange things were which filled every drawer. 'Oh! they are only Mrs. Somerville's diplomas,' said he, with a droll look of pride and amusement. Not long after this the family went abroad, partly for Dr. Somerville's health; and great has been the concern of her friends at so losing her, while it was well known that her longings were for England" (Harriet Martineau's *Autobiography*, i., p. 357).

[7] Carlyle's remarks on her will be found in his *Reminiscences*, ed. Froude, ii., p. 207; ed. Norton, i., p. 172.

is coming to introduce me to her to-morrow; and within a mile I have a *circle* of acquaintances. One of these who lives in prodigious *shine* with wife and family, you may happen to recollect something about—a grave, handsome man, who has been here repeatedly, and treats me with infinite respect, and takes immensely to my Husband—a sort of person with whom one talks about "the condition of art" in this country, and such-like topics of general interest, and studies to support the reputation of a rather intellectual and excessively reasonable woman. Can you divine who I mean? Impossible. George Rennie! How has it happened? Quite simply. I am one of the most amiable women living, tho', like your Uncle, "my virtues are unknown."

I am incapable of cherishing resentment, even against a faithless lover. I heard he was there. I wondered what he was like. I sent him my address. He came instantaneously with his sister Margaret. Bess, did I feel awkward? To be sure I did, and looked awkward, for I was within an ace of fainting, and he looked like one of his own marbles. But neither of us, I believe, entertained a particle of tenderness for the other; nevertheless, it was mere queeziness from the intense sensation of the flight of time, which such a meeting occasioned one. Fifteen years! only think! He is much improved by age, in appearance, manner, and also, I think, in character; but he lives in the wretchedest atmosphere of "*gigmanity*."[8] His wife is a perfect fool—the whole kin of them are fools—and poor George

---

[8] Carlyle's word for "respectability," "gentility." Cf. Norton, *Letters of Thomas Carlyle* [Second Series], i., p. 299: "I have a deep, irrevocable, all-comprehending Ernulphus Curse to read upon—GIGMANITY; that is the Baal Worship of this time." *Gigmania* is a variation of the word. Cf. the letter in Froude, *Thomas Carlyle*, A. ii., pp. 121, 122 (not in Norton), where he says: "God is still in Heaven, whether Henry Brougham and Jeremiah Bentham know it or not: and the gig, and gigmania must rot or start into thousand shivers, and bury itself in the ditch, that *Man* may have clean roadway towards the goal whither through all ages he is tending." In Mr. Froude's note the word is explained as an "allusion to Thurtell's trial: 'I always thought him a respectable man.' 'What do you mean by respectable?' 'He kept a gig.'" Another version makes "gentleman" the term so defined. Thurtell was the Elstree murderer (1823).

must either go in with their folly to a certain extent, or break his heart, or blow up his whole household sky-high. Moreover, he is still self-willed and vain enough to show me as often as I see him that I made an escape. I go often to Margaret's, who lives in style also, but seems to feel rather out of her element here. Lady Kinloch is close by the Rennies; she was amazed to see me, and is very kind. I am glad she is not "*dead.*"

For the rest our society, with a few additions, and [? is] much the same that we had when here formerly, only I find it much pleasanter now, being in better case for enjoying it. John Mill, Leigh Hunt, and Mrs. Austin remain my favourites. I know some Elliots, acquaintances of David Aitken, who are very agreeable people. By the by, did Mr. Aitken tell you what a frantically affectionate reception I gave him at Craigenputtoch? He looked rather fearful for the consequences to his cloth. I shall never learn to give up these outbreakings of the old woman in me from time to time. The other morning when Mr. Terrot[9] came in (who is to carry this ?), I sprang into his arms, and I believe almost stifled him with the ardour of my embrace. He returned it, however, with more sympathy than was to have been anticipated. I have wondered at my audacity ever since, for the thought of such an attempt in a cool moment would have made me quake. For God['s]sake write and tell me what everybody in Edinburgh is doing, especially my own relations, whom methinks I ought to know something about. I so seldom hear out of Scotland. My Mother is most scrupulous about putting me to the expense of postage. I shall be down perhaps next year, and then it will be hard if I do not see you. But will you never come here? I declare to Heaven there is nobody except my Mother I should welcome with such delight. After all, you are the only

---

[9] Probably the clergyman of the Scottish Episcopal Church, afterwards Bishop of Edinburgh, who is referred to in *Letters and Memorials*, ii., p. 286, and elsewhere. He had been incumbent of the "chapel" at Haddington from 1814 to 1817 (Martine, *Reminiscences of Haddington*, p. 82).

right female friend I ever had in the world—the only one I can to all lengths, and without the least misgiving, talk nonsense to—and that I consider a pretty good test of friendship. Here I must be always so *sensible*, it is really quite frightful. Carlyle wrote to your Uncle and sent a book; did he get either letter or parcel? He now sends his constant regards. God bless you, my dear Eliza. I am always, in spite of neglect in the article of writing,

Your truly attached Friend,
JANE W. CARLYLE.

You will remark again, "Jane once wrote a beautiful hand." Well, it cannot be helped; the pen is bad, and I am in haste.

Kisses without number to your Uncle. Love to your Mother.

Does old Dr. Hamilton yet live? If so, do call on him, or write him a note, and say that I am here, and love him, and am almost quite well. Is Benjamin B—— (as we hear) divorced and mad?

XLV.

To Miss Stodart, 22 George Square, Edinburgh.

[Postmark, *Feb.* 29*th*, 1836.]

DEAR, DEAR ELIZA,—

It has several times occurred to me of late, with a painful force of apprehension, that I am what is called *bewitched*. I sit here week after week, month after month, looking at things which I have the most evident call to do, and with apparently no more power to bestir myself than the Lady in *Comus!* For instance, with respect to yourself; I have wished to tell you, have meant to tell you, and by all laws of good loving ought to have told you, ages ago, that I am still alive, and true to you as in the days of my "*wee existence*"; and yet for no visible reason, I have gone on telling you nothing of the sort—nothing of *any* sort, but leaving you to suppose me a heartless renegade, unless indeed your faith be greater than that of woman. Well! believe it or no, as you like and can;

I love you still with all the *ardour of my young enthusiasm*—much more heartily and trustfully than I am apt to love nowadays with my middle-aged discretion! Yet I have set myself very seriously to the business of loving since I came here, conscious that my long sojourn in the wilderness had developed certain misanthropical tendencies in me that were leading me rather devilward—into the region of hatred and all uncharitableness! With a good deal of effort I have got up a sentiment for several men and women, which has a good right to go by the name of friendship in these days. I have even executed two or three *innocent flirtations* with good effect, and on the whole live in great amity with my fellow creatures. They call me "*sweet*," and "*gentle*"; and some of the men go the length of calling me "ENDEARING," and I laugh in my sleeve,[1] and think, Oh Lord! if you but knew what

---

[1] Here there is a very rude little sketch, in the "symbolical" stage of art, representing a female figure, whose extended fingers touch the nose.

My judicious Uncle! you were there and there a true Prophet! I have long ago learnt to distrust the ecstasies produced at sight of met & others, and consequently cease to give way to any bout of ecstasy in myself. When I fly into any raves abms nows and "swear everlasting friendship" it is always with a secret misgiving, and a dimt own almost visible consciousness of a certain theatricality in the transaction. The words 'forever' 'eternal' 'floreabint faithful' and such like applied to friendships and loves that one begins at the years of discretion never fall on my ears except accompanied by something like the distant laugh of malicious genii. Melancholy effects of age!.. "O! the days when I was young!" and conjures and foolish!

a brimstone of a creature I am behind all this beautiful amiability! But my *sentiment* for *you*, dearest, is not "*got up*," but grown up with me out of my sunny childhood, and wears always a sunny, healthful look, that these half-literary, half-sentimental intimacies, contracted after thirty, can never match. The fault, however, is not in the *people*, but in the *time*. "You great fool," said my Uncle Robert once to me, when I was flying into somebody's arms on the North Bridge, "you will surely learn some time or other that everybody is not in such ecstasies to see you as you are in to see everybody!" My judicious Uncle! you were there and then a true prophet. I have long ago learnt to distrust the ecstasies produced at sight of me in others, and consequently ceased to give way to any sort of ecstasy in myself. When I fly into any one's arms *now* and "*swear everlasting friendship*,"[2] it is always with a

---

[2] Cf. Hookham Frere's *Rovers*, Act. i., Sc. 1: "A sudden thought strikes me. Let us swear an eternal friendship." More cautious was the suggestion of a South American

secret misgiving, and a secret and almost risible conscious[ness] of a certain *theatricality* in the transaction. The words "*for ever*," "*eternal*," "*constant*," "*faithful*," and such like, applied to the friendships and loves that one *begins* at the years of discretion, never fall on my ears except accompanied by something like the distant laugh of malicious fiends. Melancholy effects of age!! "O the days when I was young!" and confident and foolish! Do *you* like to be wise, Bess? I don't at all! but one is obliged to put a good face on the matter, and so I sit here in No. 5, Cheyne Row, and make grave pantomime, and grave speech in acknowledgment of all the wisdom I hear uttered by the celebrated men and women of the age, thinking my own thought all the while, which is often this or something like this: "Was not sitting under a hay-stack[3]

---

student at Edinburgh, who, having been on a committee at the time of a rectorial election, proposed to the other members of it to "have a supper, and swear eternal friendship for three years" (the remaining part of his curriculum).

[3] Cf. Letter V., p. 21.

in a summer's day with Bess and George Rennie, or even weeping childlike, purely affectionate tears at the sound of *the Castle bugles*,[4]—when, in reply to my demand to be allowed to marry, they sent me two half-crowns and some barley-sugar,—worth a whole eternity of this idle speculation and barren logic?" But the people here are good people, and with many noble gifts in them, and to me they have been quite incomprehensibly kind, so that I ought not to feel discontent with THEM, because the magic of the *imagination* in me has got impaired by years, and no spectacles that *reason* can invent does anything at making the world so green and glorious for me as it once was. My chief intimates are a family of Sterlings: the Father, known by the name of "*the thunderer of the*

---

[4] From Letter V., it is clear the hayfield was near her home, so that Edinburgh Castle is out of the question. A Haddington correspondent tells me that "from 1803-1814 a large body of troops were stationed in Haddington in permanent barracks." Cf. Martine, *Reminiscences of Haddington*, pp. 122-127. It is probably to their bugles that Mrs. Carlyle alludes. She would be thirteen years old in 1814.

Times," a clever, tumultuous vap⁵ . . . sort of a half-Irishman; the Mother, a kind, sincere, well-enough cultivated, most motherly half-Scotchwoman; the Son! an angel of Heaven—*ostensibly* a Clergyman of the Church of England, and Author of *Arthur Coningsby*, a highly original novel; he has also a wife, very fat and good-natured and fine-ladyish in the *best* sense of the term. These people, as the elder Sterling told Susan Hunter when she was here, "*all adore me.*" Certainly they load me with kindnesses, and treat me as if I were a sort of necessary to their existence. The very footman and lady's-maid "have been quite anxious" if I have stayed away half a week. Mrs. Sterling's portrait in oil hangs over my mantlepiece, and the whole thing is in the most flourishing condition, if it do but last. Then I have an Italian Conte,⁶ one of the first poets of Italy,

---

⁵ Part of the word destroyed by the seal. *Query* "vapouring"?

⁶ "Pepoli has been twice, and is gliding into a flirtation with—*mia madre!* who presented him, in a manner *molto*

the handsomest and best mannered of men, who comes twice a week or so and makes my thoughts melodious for the rest of the day. He was my Mother's chief, indeed I think *only*, favourite here among all our people; which was curious, as they had no medium of communication but their eyes! For my part, I speak Italian now like a nightingale, and *will*, I am told, soon write it "*better* than any native Signora"! Like the man and the fiddle, nobody knows what he can do till he try. Did you hear tell of my Darling Degli Antoni?[7] your recent distress prevented me introducing her to you among the rest of my Edinburgh friends. She is another of my special friends; it is so delightful to be called "*carissima amica*," etc.,

---

graziosa, with her tartan scarf" (Letter to her husband of October 12th, 1835: *Letters and Memorials*, i. p. 35). "Il Conte 'Pepoli,'" says Carlyle, "was from Bologna, exile and dilettante, a very pretty man; married, some years hence, Elizabeth Fergus of Kirkcaldy (elderly, moneyed, and fallen in love with the romantic in distress); and now, as widower, lives in Bologna again" (*ib*. p. 33).

[7] Cf. *Letters and Memorials*, i., p. 27.

etc., that it is worth while to keep up an Italian friendship or two for the purpose. But oh, my dear Eliza, would you but come and *see* all that I have, in the way of friends, in the way of house room, in the way of heart room! What glorious days we might still have together, after all that is come and gone! Your Uncle, I rejoice to hear, is better again; can you not come then? the journey is a mere trifle, the welcome would be a great reality! To me you would indeed be welcome as flowers in May, or rather were it not better to say as flowers in December; and to my Husband you would be welcome, as a cigar in a land destitute of tobacco!! O Bess, will you, will you come? Kisses to your Uncle. My Husband is pretty well, almost thro' the second volume of his ill-fated book;[8] thinks of your Uncle and you with grateful affection,—is on the whole the cleverest man I meet with still and the truest.

---

[8] *The French Revolution*, vol. i. of which had been burnt, and had to be all rewritten. See *Reminiscences*, ed. Norton, i., p. 106, *note;* Froude, *Thomas Carlyle*, B. i., p. 27.

I have never yet thanked you with my own hand[9] for your beautiful stockings, but I never wear them without thanking you silently. God bless you, Dearest. Write to me soon, tho' I do not deserve it, and love me always.

Your own

JANE WELSH.[10]

---

[9] Cf. p. 223, Letter XXXVII., *note* 2.
[10] *Sic.*

XLVI.

[Eliza Stodart was married on July 13th, 1836, to David Aitken. I have found no letter from Mrs. Carlyle to her on the occasion, though it is likely that there was one.]

Mrs. D. Aitken, Minto Manse, Hawick.

[Postmark, *March 6th*, 1837.]

Dearest Eliza,—

Your husband's letter written in Influenza found me in the same.[1] I have had it severely and long, and am only now getting out in the heat of the day (if there be any such thing); while my head, when it does not absolutely ache, continues to feel much as if it had been brayed in a mortar. Happily, myself and the cat are the only individuals that have been laid up in this house; and as neither it nor I have anything at press, or are acting upon the public in any particular way, "the prevailing malady" could

---

[1] Cf. Froude, *Thomas Carlyle*, B. i., p. 100; *Letters and Memorials*, i., p. 64 ff. For "Influenza," cf. Letter LI., *note* 1.

not have made a more judicious election. Indeed, I would rather have the whole to do over again a dozen times myself, than that my husband should have anything to say to it at present; he is so worried with other matters. Two printers are on his book at the same time, and the life he leads between them puts me in mind of those unhappy "*fish, fish*" in the *Arabian Nights* that were always a-frying and required to be "*at their duty*." [2] Besides this, he has a course of lectures on German Literature[3] hanging over him, which it is evident to me he will not have an hour's leisure to prepare, and how he is to get thro' them successfully without preparation, or what is to become of poor me if he break down in the midst, are questions of no light concern to my forecasting mind. But "I hope better things tho' I thus speak." A lady was suggesting to me the other day that the danger of all dangers for him would

---

[2] "Story of the Fisherman." In Lane's translation the words run: "O fish, fish, are ye remaining faithful to your covenant?"

[3] Cf. Froude, *Thomas Carlyle*, B. i., p. 97 ff.

be at the very outset, that if he only escaped saying "Gentlemen and Ladies," instead of "Ladies and Gentlemen," the rest would be all plain sailing. And he promised that he will certainly say neither the one thing nor the other.[4] So I await what May shall bring forth with tolerable composure; the more, as it is the people who have asked HIM to speak, rather than he who has asked the people to hear. When the Book [5] is done with, and the Lectures done with, he proposes going to Scotland or somewhere for a long rest. But I do not think of accompanying him, having almost a cat-like attachment to my own house, as well as a constitutional incapacity for travelling, to say nothing of the preference I give to London before all other places. It is, in fact, a jewel of a place, for this reason, that if you want to be solitary you may have your humour out as completely as if you were at Craigenputtoch, and if you are socially disposed you may have society to all

---

[4] Cf. *Letters and Memorials*, i., p. 72.

[5] *The French Revolution*. It was published in this year (1837).

lengths and of every possible *cut*, so that it is strange if you do not find something to suit you. For my part, I go upon the principle that variety is charming; and as somebody was telling me of myself the other day, I have a whole *humanum genus* (human race) of friends.

In fact, if there is any one thing to be learnt more than another by living in London, it is a due Catholicism of taste. One sees so many things which one has been used to consider antagonist and irreconcilable existing alongside of one another in peace and harmony; and still more one learns to *lassen gelten*[6] (ask your Husband—happy that you have one who knows German), by the fair appreciation *you* find from people as different as possible from yourself and from one another. Never has it happened to me to hear in London that phrase which in small towns, and even in Edinburgh, one is constantly hearing: such and such people "are not in *my* way."

---

[6] *Lit.* "allow to have value," "to let pass (as current coin)." It should be *gelten lassen*.

People are content here with simply *having* ways, without trying to persuade their neighbours that they are the only ones that lead to salvation. They have ascertained that from the centre to the circumference there are many more radii than one, and they are only moved to astonishment and disapprobation when a fellow-creature flies *over the circumference* into the infinite Inane. But this is unbearable, to philosophize and metaphorize all in a breath! You will agree, however, that it is not easy to keep oneself "*a plain human creature*" in the midst of so much example to the contrary. Positively for weeks together, sometimes, I do not set eyes on or exchange words with one "plain human creature," but only with human creatures more or less ornamented, or— perverted. Of all these ornamented human creatures the one I take most delight in is Harriet Martineau. The horrid picture in *Fraser*[7] with

---

[7] Vol. viii. (1833), p. 576. It is a frightful caricature— especially the cat. [These portraits and notices have been republished in 1874 and 1883.] Cf. Froude, *Thomas Carlyle*, B. i., p. 97; *Reminiscences*, ed. Froude, ii., pp. 212–

the cat looking over its shoulder was not a bit like; and the Artist deserved to have been hanged and quartered for so vile a calumny. Neither does the idea generally formed of the woman merely from her reputation as a *Political Economist* do her more justice than that picture! They may call her what they please, but it is plain to me and to everybody of common sense (as my Uncle Robert said) that she is distinctly good-looking, warm-hearted even to a pitch of romance, witty as well as wise, very entertaining and entertainable in spite of the deadening and killing appendage of an ear-trumpet, and finally, as "our Mother" used to finish off a good character, "*very fond of* ME." I had a fly at Fanny Kemble (Mrs. Butler)[8] also this winter, but it would not do. She is Green-room all over, and with a heart all tossed up into blank verse—blank verse, too,

---

217; ed. Norton, i., pp. 176-180; *Correspondence of Carlyle and Emerson*, i., p. 126. For Miss Martineau's impressions of the Carlyles and their circle, cf. her *Autobiography*, i., pp. 377-387.

[8] Cf. *Letters and Memorials*, i., p. 67; Harriet Martineau's *Autobiography*, i., p. 365.

of the "fish—be it ev'—er so salt, is ne'—er too salt for me" sort. The longer I live, the more I want naturalness in people. I think Mr. Simpson would say I keep "my charming naïveté"[9] to a wonder.

I have filled my paper without a word on the subject nearest *your* heart, and nearest mine while I have been writing.[10] But I do as I would be done by. I offer no idle condolences, for I never found such of any comfort to myself, and my regard for your Uncle is well enough known to you to make any assurances of sympathy from *me* superfluous. I hoped to have seen him again. It was not to be. He is gone from us all, but the memory of his worth and his kindness will abide with some of us while we live.

I should have written this to your Husband, but it is not lost what a friend gets. Perhaps, too, I

---

[9] Cf. Letter XLI., p. 248.

[10] According to his tombstone in the Greyfriars' Churchyard, Edinburgh, "John Bradfute died 16th January, 1837, aged seventy-three." Sam. Aitken, who died October 4th, 1847, is buried beside him.

should have written it more legibly, but "*the weather is cold, and I am grown old,*" and so I have the paper on my knees in front of the fire, which is not a way to make copperplate. Pray write soon, for I am anxious to hear that your health is quite restored.

Your affectionate

JANE CARLYLE.

XLVII.

[No address preserved.—To the Rev. David Aitken.]

CHELSEA,
8 *Septr.*, 1840.

MY DEAR SIR,—

This morning, by the "Parcels Delivery Company," there was duly put into my hand a copy of Peterkin's *Booke of the Universal Kirk*,[1] the *origin* of which phenomenon, as I find by the fly-leafe[2] of said *Booke*, is well known to you! Every phenomenon has its origin. There are certain companies in which [it] is not very safe to speak; if you speak, none can warrant you but

---

[1] *The Booke of the Universall Kirk of Scotland : wherein the headis and conclusionis devysit be the ministers and commissionaris of the particular kirks thereof are specially expressed and contained.* Edited by Alexander Peterkin, Esq., late Sheriff-substitute of Orkney. Edin. 1839. [The full title of this book, which is not in the Bodleian Library, has been kindly sent me by Mr. G. K. Fortescue, of the British Museum, to whom I am also indebted for *note* 5 on Letter XLVIII.].

[2] *Sic.*

straightway it shall be done! I return many kind thanks. I have already taken a day's reading out of the *Booke*; and expect to read it all, with a pleasure increased by the way in which it comes to me.

You are in the pleasant vale of Esk by this time; or perhaps almost home at Minto. May good go with you both; and peaceful pleasant days await you among the Hills! My own movement Northward is vaguer than ever, perhaps doubtful now altogether. I am sick, the weather is cold; like Sterne's Starling, one has to say mournfully, "I can't get out!" [3]

We unite in many kind wishes to you and Mrs. Aitken. I remain always

Yours very truly

T. CARLYLE.

---

[3] Cf. p. 19, Letter V., *note* 1. Carlyle introduces the Starling into his *Frederick the Great*, book xi., chap. i. (vol. iii., p. 37, in original edition).

XLVIII.

[*No address preserved.—To the Rev. David Aitken.*]

CHELSEA,
9 *Decr.*, 1840.

MY DEAR SIR,—

Partly connected with the *Booke of the Kirk*, which you were kind enough to leave me as a legacy when you last went hence, there is another Book, *Baillie's Letters and Journals*,[1] which I want very greatly to get, and cannot fall in with here for love or money. I have looked on it in the *British Museum*, but it is beyond my faculty to read it there; and nowhere else, in Bookshops, Cambridge Libraries,[2] or the shelves of private friends, can I discover more than traditions and provoking rumours of it. I am told the Book is common in Scotland: who knows but you may have it, or may in some way have access to it, and could let me have a loan of it for a

---

[1] See *note* 2 on next letter.
[2] Cf. Froude, *Thomas Carlyle*, B. i., p. 152.

little? I boast of the virtue of returning books lent me, in a faithful manner! Our friend Sam could easily find means of conveyance,—to the care of Fraser in Regent Street. On the whole, letters being so cheap[3] and you so helpful, I find I may at least ask you about it.—Literary men borrow books *sub rosâ*, it is said, from the Advocates' and Signet and all manner of open Libraries, and have them sent hither and sent thither, punctually restoring them; it is a thing not entirely unknown to myself of old; but I am out of all their Ledgers there for a long while past.

Baillie's is not the only Book I want; the History of Scotch Covenanting, which is the History of Scotland altogether in Charles *First's* time, is the point I drive at. Much that perhaps is common in Edinburgh is unattainable here. Did not some "Stevenson"[4] or other lately put

---

[3] Penny postage had been introduced on January 10th of this year.

[4] Carlyle probably refers to *The History of the Church and State of Scotland from the Accession of King Charles*

forth a publication on that subject? I have now by me a very trivial *History of the Covenanters*, published by Waugh and Innes in 1830, two small volumes;[5] but it tells me nothing which I did not long ago know, or even know the contrary of. Did Peterkin promulgate nothing on this? Do no Pamphets, Records, State Trials

---

I. *to the Restoration of King Charles II.*, in 4 vols., by Andrew Stevenson (the editor of Baillie's *Letters*. See p. 298, Letter XLIX, *note* 2). Only three vols. actually appeared (1753-1757), bringing the work down to 1649. Principal Fairbairn has shown me an edition, "complete in one volume" (with "*the year* 1649" substituted in the title for "*the Restoration of King Charles II.*"), published by T. Nelson (Edin., 1840), without any indication that it is merely a reprint of an old book; and this has probably misled Carlyle, who has only heard of it, into the use of the term "lately." It is possible, but less likely, that he may have heard of some of the works published by Thomas G. Stevenson, of Princes Street, Edinburgh. In a catalogue of his of 1848 are several books relating to ecclesiastical affairs in Scotland in the Seventeenth Century, published between 1825 and 1840; e.g. *Biographia Presbyteriana* and *Historical Fragments relative to Scotch Affairs from* 1635-1664.

[5] *History of the Covenanters in Scotland.* By the author of the *Histories of the Reformation, Christian Church*, etc. [William Sime]. 2 vols. Edinburgh, 12mo.

or the like exist, which can help one to represent to himself those actual Scottish years from 1637–1660, especially the earlier portion of them? What for example, *is* known about Jenny Geddes and her performance in St. Giles's in that summer Sunday of 1637? Do not laugh, I pray you; but ask some Dr. Lee[6] or other, if so be any Dr. can tell. You will oblige me greatly. Poor old *Spalding*[7] is but a kind of triviality; yet he is worth all the rest to me hitherto. I read Mark Napier's first Book on *Montrose*[8] too,— with astonishment, confusion and despair. What I learnt of new was the colour of Montrose's stockings when they hanged him; this and almost

---

[6] Dr. Lee became Principal of Edinburgh University in this year. "Archdeacon Meadows," in Hill Burton's *Book-Hunter*, is a kindly caricature of him.

[7] John Spalding's *History of the Troubles and Memorable Transactions in Scotland*, 1624–45, was published in 2 vols., Aberdeen, 1792, and republished by the Bannatyne Club in 1828–1829 (also by the Spalding Club in 1850).

[8] Napier's "first book on *Montrose*" must mean his *Montrose and the Covenanters*, London, 1838. In this year (1840) he published *The Life and Times of Montrose* (Edin.). Napier was a vehement defender of the Royalist side.

nothing more from Mark. In short, I am very ill off indeed; and could be right thankful for charitable help from any quarter of the sky.

Did you ever see the young man D——? He wrote me a long letter, in my answer to which I inserted a card to introduce him if he liked. No word since. I am interested in this forlorn D——, and find traces of a valiant, substantial heart in him; a man perhaps *capable* of being helped (which so few are), if one knew how! It is a divine office; the divinest we have here below, that of helping. Tell me whether I have procured you such a luxury in this man's acquaintance; or only a new trouble and futility.

My Wife is better than usual this winter: we join in many cordial salutations to you and Mrs. A.

Yours always truly,
T. CARLYLE.

XLIX.

[*No address preserved.—To the Rev. David Aitken.*]

CHELSEA, 22 *Feb.*, 1841.

MY DEAR SIR,—

Above two months ago I was on the point of writing to you, and ought not to have heeded the fallacious whispers of Indolence, but actually to have written, that *Baillie's Letters* had actually come into my possession. A certain Dr. Murray,[1] an early acquaintance of mine in Edinburgh, happened to possess the Book; and lent it me for an unlimited time. I have read it; with unusual interest and profit. One wonders that such a Book ever fell into such a state of rarity, of unprocurability. It is scandalously edited too, or

---

[1] "Thomas Murray [one of Carlyle's early correspondents] became a minister, wrote a respectable literary history of Galloway, his native county, was for a time editor of the *Edinburgh Weekly Chronicle*, and lived to a good old age." —Prof. Norton, *Early Letters of Thomas Carlyle*, i., p. ix. He wrote a *Life of Samuel Rutherford* (*ib.*, ii., p. 360), and would thus be specially interested in Scotch history of the seventeenth century.

rather not edited at all, only printed,—and that also in an entirely scandalous manner.—The Bannatyne people, I am very glad to find, are getting out a proper reprint of *Baillie*, to be accompanied with Notes.² He is a great blockhead B., but he carried a pair of eyes in his head; which so few do. I have got *Turner*³ from Cambridge; I can get a variety of things: but all that has been suspended for some time with Proofsheets⁴ and chaotic *etceteras*.

What you say of D—— corresponds pretty exactly with all I have been able to learn or surmise about him. The other day he sends me a most tumultuous, boisterous explosion of a letter; good in the heart of it, something almost like *genius* in the heart of it; but wild as the woods.

---

² Baillie's *Letters* were printed at Edinburgh in 3 vols. small 8vo, 1753–1757, edited by Andrew Stevenson. They were edited by David Laing for the Bannatyne Club in 3 vols., in 1841.

³ *Memoirs of his own Life and Times*, by Sir James Turner, 1632–1670; published by the Bannatyne Club in 1829.

⁴ Of the Lectures *On Heroes*.

Such an Orson will take terrible shaving and tawing!

On the whole, I wish you saw the man, to report about him. A poor brother struggling in that same Orson-state, if he be aidable at all, appeals to one. Help is due to the help-needing! I want your report about D—— as soon as you can.

We are not ill here; glad in some gleams of returning Spring. The tumult of London, ever onwards from this season, gets triple and tenfold; more and more hateful to me, fatal to me. Were the weather once warm, I seriously meditate running off somewhither.

We unite in all kind regards to Mrs. Aitken. As for you, you must take care of the Edinburgh East-winds. It is a serious sad fate to be "seldom free from pain";—to be never free from it: ah me!—

Commend us also in the kindest manner to our right trusty and well beloved Sam.

Yours always truly
T. CARLYLE.

L.

[*No address preserved.—To Mrs. Aitken, Minto.*]
[The letter enclosed is dated *March* 30*th*, 1841.]

5 CHEYNE ROW, CHELSEA.

MY DEAR ELIZA,—

We have Scripture for it: "Woe unto you when all men speak well of you!" but when one man speaks extravagantly well of you—*that* I hope does not imply *woe*, otherwise your husband and you run a terrible risk! It seems to me that I should be very hard-hearted, if I suffered the flowery raptures of that enthusiastic Mr. D—— to be turned to the baseness of *setting* tallow candles, etc., etc.; and as to laying them by with select letters, I should be afraid of their igniting the whole mass, so I enclose them to you, whom they chiefly concern. I advise you to put them under glass in a frame, and hang them up over your sideboard, as George Rennie did with an address from some borough, which was ambitious of having him for its representative in Parliament.

By the way, George Rennie has been here

three times within the last ten days, which I impute to his having had Influenza. Illness softens his heart always, and in rendering the present extremely disgusting to him, inclines him to seek consolation from the *past*. The same phenomena occurred after his smallpox.

For the rest we are going on here much in the old way. Severe as the winter was, it did not reach my chest; I "took *time* by the forelock," (do you remember him?) and shut myself up *before* being ill, which saved me from becoming ill. Some weeks ago I was taken to bed with a sore throat, which I cured myself by flaying it pretty effectually with a blister. Helen declared I "should never be *fit to be seen* in this world again;" but it mended in no time, and now merely looks excessively *dirty*, and dirty necks in London are much more frequent than clean ones. Carlyle *growls* along, but does no practical mischief[1]—the most unmanageable feature of his

---

[1] In a letter to Carlyle's mother (autumn, 1840) she says: "Carlyle is reading voraciously [about Cromwell, etc.], preparatory to writing a new book. For the rest, he growls

actual manner of being is that he is always crying out to be away somewhere, and never goes. His portmanteau has been standing on a chair, half packed, for the last four weeks, with a direction on it—Mr. Carlyle, *Passenger*—— but passenger in *what*, or *whither*, no man, least of all himself, has the faintest idea; and if I were required, with a loaded pistol at my breast, to fill up the card, the only thing I could put with a shadow of probability would be passenger into Infinite space![2] What is to become of us thro'-out the summer I know as little. "White men know nothing";[3] white women less than nothing. God bless you, anyhow.

Ever your affectionate
JANE CARLYLE.

---

away much in the old style; but one gets to feel a certain indifference to his growling; if one did not, it would be the worse for one" (*Letters and Memorials*, i., p. 126).

[2] He did finally go to "Milnes's [R. Monckton Milnes, afterwards Lord Houghton], at Fryston in Yorkshire" (*Letters and Memorials*, i., p. 132, *note* 1).

[3] Allusion unknown. It may be something in a novel. A correspondent tells me he remembers reading of some Australian native, who says, "White fellow, foolish fellow."

LI.

[This and the following letter I am allowed to print by the kind permission of R. Scot Skirving, Esq. Letter LI. was written to his aunt about him, and Letter LII. is one of several which were written by Mrs. Carlyle to himself. Mr. Skirving gives me a most interesting account of the first time he saw Mrs. Carlyle, who was a friend of his family. "When a schoolboy," he says, "I was one day following the congenial occupation of robbing sparrows' nests in the ruined portion of the grand old church of Haddington—'The Lantern of the Lothians'—when, to my horror, I saw Mrs. Carlyle come and seat herself on her father's tombstone (which is flat), and then she bowed her head and prayed and meditated for at least half-an-hour. I hesitated a moment, when she came, whether to make myself known, and be over with it; but I preferred to slink into a corner close up to the wall, and there I stood during the whole time she remained. I recognised her, because I had heard my mother and aunt talk about her, and I knew she was staying with her friends, the Donaldsons. I afterwards heard she had been that day to visit the old church." Mr. Skirving thinks the date of this visit must have been 1833 or 1834. It would seem extremely probable that Mrs. Carlyle should have gone out from Edinburgh, where she was staying in the spring of 1833 (see p. 227 ff.), to visit Haddington. I find no trace of her having been in the east of Scotland in the spring of 1834, before the removal to London. Mr. Froude must be in error, when he says that Mrs. Carlyle never revisited Haddington after her marriage until 1849 (*Letters and Memorials*, ii., p. 51, *note*).]

[*To Miss Scot of Haddington.*]

5, Cheyne Row,

Wednesday.

[Spring of 1841.]

My dear Miss Scot,—

Your letter found me in bed, transacting that abomination to which they have given the mellifluous Italian name *Influenza*[1]—the hardest mouthful of German gutturals would better suit it. But it would lead one into endless quarrel with the world if one should insist on everything going by its right name: so let Influenza remain Influenza; and many other things besides *sound* musically, so that an unexperienced person would almost desire to have them, while they *are*—what

---

[1] *Influenza* received its name because Italian physicians ascribed the epidemic to the influence of the stars. See Art. in *Encyc. Brit.* (9th edit.).

we know. What I had to tell you, more to the purpose, is, that I got out of bed a day sooner than I should otherwise have done for fear of missing your young Hopeful; and this is fact, and not *blarney*. He had sent on the letter by post, with no other indication of his whereabouts than the tolerably vague one contained in the postmark 'Cheapside'; so I expected from day to day that he would come to justify this unnatural proceeding. But no; and now it is so long, that I fear he is actually gone on his way, and I am not to see him at all. This is really a considerable *bêtise* which the young gentleman has committed at the very outset of his travels. There was Giovanni Ruffini,[2] asking me continually 'was

---

[2] Author of *Doctor Antonio* and other English novels. *Lorenzo Benoni* is partly autobiographical. The Ruffinis were connected with Mazzini in the Association of "Young Italy." One of them, Jacopo, to escape the moral torture inflicted by Charles Albert's government, opened a vein in his neck with a nail from the door of his prison, and "with this last protest against tyranny," says Mazzini, "he took refuge in the bosom of his Creator." Mazzini came to London in 1837.

X

he come?' having been instructed by his brother in Edinburgh to show him all the second-hand *gratitude* in his power to show; and Mazzini himself, the first of Italian men, the young chief of *Giovane Italia*, had offered me some letters for him, to Florence and elsewhere. And then, only think of the stupidity of not coming to see my Husband! one of the most popular London sights at present, which *he* might have seen '*for nothing*'; not to speak of the interest which he ought to have felt in myself, who knew him before he was born, and whom he must all his life have heard tell of as an ornament to Humanity!

By the time he comes back from Italy, he will have learned, it is to be hoped, to look a little sharper to his own interests. Meanwhile, what can one do but recommend him to Providence?

I wish you had come along with him to see him safe out of the kingdom; not that I have any fears about his safety, but that I should like to have had you here, and I know that people so *rational* as you are never *fatigue* themselves, except for the benefit of others. If you who saw me in the

Desert saw me in Chelsea, you would admit that never was a poor woman so tried between "fierce extremes";[3] and I would like you should, that I might have a confidential fit of laughter with you over this melodramatic life which has been appointed me to live here below, or a fit of crying, whichever you liked best.

But among all the people I see it is so seldom I look upon a face that speaks to me of long ago—so seldom I hear a voice with a tone of home in it. The few people I know here connected with Haddington are so *disconnected*, so incompatible with the sort of thing we live in, that I have long since renounced all attempts *to piece them into it*. James Aitken makes me a visit once a year or so, and brings me news tolerably out of date; and George Rennie, whom I have more of, looks always so out of humour when I speak of East Lothian!—as is natural perhaps in *him*.

---

[3] "Thither, by harpy-footed Furies haled,
  At certain revolutions all the damned
  Are brought; and feel by turns the bitter change
  Of fierce extremes, extremes by change more fierce," etc.
    Milton's *Paradise Lost*, ii., 596 ff.

Ann Veitch and her brother James called for me two days ago, and I had not seen them for two years. Ann looks *worn*, poor soul, but not *broken ;* looks as if she made a good fight against bad luck: and I have no doubt but she does. Captain Veitch, or (as my maid announced him, familiar with foreign names,[4] and taking him on the strength of his own pronunciation for some Russian), Mr. *Keppenwitch*, seems to me since I saw him last to have been "*learning himself to be gay*,"[5] the result, like such attempts [at] the falsifying [of] nature, is rather *odd*, to say the least of it.

---

[4] "Sprinklings of Foreigners, 'Political Refugees,' had already begun to come about us. . . . Only two of them had any charm for me as men: Mazzini . . . and Godefroi Cavaignac."—Carlyle, *Reminiscences*, ed. Froude, ii., pp. 181, 182 ; ed. Norton, i., p. 110.

[5] Cf. the story told by Boswell " of a heavy German baron, who had lived much with the young English at Geneva, and was ambitious to be as lively as they ; with which view, he, with assiduous exertion, was jumping over the tables and chairs in his lodgings ; and when the people of the house ran in and asked, with surprize, what was the matter, he answered '*Sh' apprens t'etre fif.'* "—Boswell's *Johnson*, Dr. G. B. Hill's edition, ii., p. 462.

I do not know what Augustine Ruffini wrote *to* you, but I know that *of* you he wrote such things as I, who do not myself deal in *couleur de rose*, should feel it indecent to repeat. Had Margaret read the letter which he wrote to *me* about your treatment of him, your manner of being, etc., etc., she would have proposed sending him *two* turkeys, or even *three*. I thank you for that little notice of her; it brought all the woman before me better than the best drawn picture could have done. How I should like to assist at the eating of one of the said turkeys! Some day perhaps I may. The first summer I am in Scotland I WILL go to Haddington, whether this summer or no is uncertain. Here is somebody come to take me a drive—*Erasmus Darwin :*[6] not the old doctor, of course, but his Grandson, who

---

[6] The elder brother of Charles Darwin, " to whom," says Carlyle, " I rather prefer him for intellect, had not his health quite doomed him to silence and patient idleness ;—Grandsons both of the first *famed* Erasmus ('Botanic Garden,' etc.) . . . My Dear One had a great favour for this honest Darwin always; many a road, to shops and the like, he drove her in his Cab ('*Darwingium Cabbum*,' compara-

is the best friend I have here—in fact, the likest thing to a brother I ever had in the world, not even excepting my brother-in-law.

Moreover, my pen is practically protesting against writing any more.

Give my love to all the people. Do write to me when you are idle and would do a good action.

Affectionately yours,
JANE CARLYLE.

---

ble to *Georgium Sidus*) in those early days, when even the charge of Omnibuses was a consideration."—*Reminiscences*, ed. Froude, ii., p. 208; ed. Norton, i., p. 173.

LII.

[Mr. Scot Skirving thinks the date of this letter must be 1847; but I have placed it here because of its connexion with the preceding. The letter which Mrs. Carlyle wrote to him in 1841 (referred to in this, p. 313), Mr. Skirving is unable to find; but he recollects some parts very distinctly. It began: "My dear ——, what on earth shall I call you? '*Robert*' to one I never saw seems odd; yet what else can I call a man I knew before he was born? So you passed through London on your way to Italy and did not come to see me! It was very wrong of you. I am exactly the sort of woman a young man ought to know. I would have done you much good." Then followed a description of herself. In concluding she said: "My husband carried me last summer to a vile place on the shore of the Solway, where I could think of nothing by day for the eternal moan-moaning of the sea, and nothing by night for industrious fleas." The "place on the Solway" was Annan. See *Correspondence of Carlyle and Emerson*, i., pp. 336, 337.]

[*To Robert Scot Skirving, Esq.*]

5 CHEYNE ROW, CHELSEA,
11*th May* [1847 ?].

MY DEAR—*Robert*, then, since you protest against "Sir" and "Mr."

When your letter came I was in the

country, for a week; and my maid, after her fashion of doing precisely what she is told to do —neither more nor less—kept all my letters during that time lying on the table *here*, I, in the unbounded confidence of my nature, having given her no *express injunction* to forward them. Since my return *two days* ago, the head of me has been "too bad *for anything*" (as the Lancashire phrase is), aching in fact as if it were about giving birth to a young "*Sin*" or young "*Wisdom*,"[1] all thro' having come part of the way by steamboat in a straw bonnet that cost *two shillings*. I give you these particulars, that you may see I have lost no time that could be helped. To-day I am rather better, and write to you the first thing I do. I am glad that you are coming to London, especially since you have got over the crisis of "detestability."[2] It would have gone against my feelings to have detested you, and I

---

[1] Cf. Milton's *Paradise Lost* ii., 747 ff., where *Sin* reminds *Satan* how she sprang from his aching head "a goddess armed" (like Minerva from the head of Jove).

[2] See *Sartor Resartus*, book ii., chap. iv.

could not have helped it had I seen you in your "first pangs of finding"—that is to say *fearing* "you were to be nobody and nothing." One only begins to be really *something* after those pangs have been happily transacted; it is a sort of moral *cutting of one's teeth*.

My No. is 5, and my street spells itself *Cheyne* Row; and there is even, contrary to London etiquette, a brass plate with the name upon the door. A Chelsea omnibus will bring you within a gunshot for *sixpence*, or you may come by steamboat at the easy rate of *twopence!* If with all these helps you fail to arrive at me with perfect ease you must be the stupidest of mortals. When you come, let it be early; after one, everybody here goes out to call for everybody, everybody wishing to find everybody "not at home." How you will *like* me when you see me heaven knows. *Realised ideals*[3] are always dreadfully precarious. Nor do I remember the least in the

---

[3] "Realised Ideals" is the title of book i., chap. ii., in Carlyle's *French Revolution*.

world what sort of a sketch of myself I gave you in '41. Most likely it was wide of the mark; would depend more on *how I had slept* the previous night than on "the fact of things." My views of myself are a sort of "dissolving views," never the same for many minutes together. To-day, for example, I find myself horrid—in a second epoch of *detestability*. Our next-door neighbour having given a ball last night, the noise of which thro' the thin partition kept me awake till six in the morning; and so to-day I am in a state of "protest and appeal to Posterity"[4] against everybody and everything, my-

---

[4] The same phrase is used in a letter of Aug., 1842, in *Letters and Memorials*, i., p. 169. Carlyle in a note says that the allusion is to a story of Cavaignac's about a drunken man, who exclaimed, when boys were annoying him: "Vous êtes des injustes; je m'en appelle à la postérité." It should also be noticed that "protest and appeal" is an echo from the Scotch ecclesiastical courts. When an appeal is made from a kirk session to a presbytery, or from a presbytery to a synod, or from a synod to the General Assembly, the aggrieved member "protests and appeals and craves extracts," and must "table his shilling" (to pay for official extracts from the minutes).

self included. Will you tell your Father that one day not long ago, in a roomful of people, Frank Charteris [5] happening to name your Father, *apropos* of something about farming, I shouted out in the joyfullest tone, " Oh, dear me ! " which caused quite a sensation ?

My kindest love to your Mother and Aunt. How I should like to see them all again ! I often meditate going to survey once more with bodily eyes what is still all vivid enough in memory; but when it comes to the point my courage fails me : [6] and so,

Yours with great faith,

JANE CARLYLE.

---

[5] Afterwards Earl of Wemyss.

[6] Mrs. Carlyle revisited Haddington in 1849. See *Letters and Memorials*, ii. 51 ff.

[Mr. Skirving went, in accordance with this and other invitations, to call on the Carlyles, but found the lion in a very growling mood. After he had sat and talked with Mrs. Carlyle and Miss Jewsbury, who was with her, for some time, Carlyle entered " in a flowered dressing-gown, and a pipe a foot long." Mr. Skirving happening to mention that his mother and he had been reading Disraeli's last novel, "Then," said Carlyle, "your mother and you are fools."

"You cannot deny," answered Mr. Skirving, "that he is a great speaker, if not a great novelist."

"Young *maan*," replied Carlyle, "I hope you will live to get sense, and learn that words are no good at all; it is deeds, and deeds only."

Mr. Skirving, not feeling inclined to give way blindly to this utterance of the oracle, appositely quoted from a translation of the *Philoctetes* of Sophocles the passage where Ulysses says to Neoptolemus (l. 96 ff.):

> "Son of a noble sire! I too in youth
> Had a slow tongue and an impatient arm;
> But now, time-tried, I see in words, not deeds,
> The universal ruler of mankind."

These lines Mr. Skirving, as he still well remembers, quoted with the preface, "You do not agree with one of the wisest of the Greeks, Mr. Carlyle."

"I see what you are now," thundered Carlyle, "a damned impudent whelp of an Edinburgh Advocate!" (a mistaken inference.)

Carlyle became more kindly after this, went with his visitor to the door, and held his hand some time at parting. Mr. Skirving met Mrs. Carlyle afterwards in Scotland, and she apologized for Carlyle's treatment of him; but he never saw Carlyle again till he stood beside him, as a pall-bearer at Mrs. Carlyle's funeral in the ruined chancel of "the Lantern of the Lothians," where he had first seen her, when she visited her father's grave.]

LIII.

[Mrs. Welsh died in February, 1842. According to Carlyle's *Reminiscences* (ed. Froude, ii., p. 194; ed. Norton, i., p. 122) she died on Feb. 20th. But, according to Carlyle's note in *Letters and Memorials*, i., p. 141, she died on Feb. 26th. The account there is much more circumstantial, and is *apparently* followed by Mr. Froude in his *Life of Carlyle*, B. i., pp. 233, 234. Probably the date in the *Reminiscences* is a slip or a misreading.]

To Mrs. Aitken, Minto Manse, Hawick.

5 CHEYNE ROW,
Friday [Postmark, *June* 3*rd*, 1842].

MY DEAR ELIZA,—

I *know* that I wrote *part* of a letter to you some few weeks ago, immediately after receiving your last; but whether I finished it and sent it off, or whether it shared the fate of many others of my late undertakings and came to an untimely close, I cannot remember, tho' it were to save my life. From this you may infer that my memory is tolerably bad; indeed, all about me has been tolerably bad this long while, and I do not feel as if I could ever gather myself up into the old state again in this world. Parted as I had been from my Mother so many years, and with so many new objects of interest about me, it was not to have been foreseen that her loss could have so completely changed the whole face of my existence; indeed, I had never thought about losing her—her life seemed always better than my own. What I had thought about, and always the longer the more anxiously, was getting her beside me again, that I might show her more love and care in her old age than in the thoughtlessness of my heart I had done heretofore; and she had promised me not to keep me unquiet by passing any more winters in that lonely place—had just promised me that, "if it pleased God we should meet this summer, it should be all arranged according to my wish." So many fine schemes I had in my head for her future comfort!—too late, for her death was already on her, and I did not know it. She had taken every pains, and forced those about her to take every pains, to keep me in ignorance of her state—" a journey at that season would be so dangerous for me!" All her last weeks seemed one continued thought about *me*—to ward off anxiety from me while she lived, and to soften the shock for me should she die. In a letter she wrote to Dr. Russel[1], after many directions about what was to be done for me if I *must* be sent for, she concluded with these words, which stick for ever in my heart: "For Jeannie must be saved in *every* way, or there is much to be dreaded." And when the first stroke came upon her, Margaret Macqueen being by, she uttered no thought for her own future, only in sinking down exclaimed, "I am dying, Margaret! Oh, my poor Jeannie " On the Saturday I received a letter from her—tender and cheerful as all her late letters had been. She had written the day before, she said, and had nothing new to tell me. But as there was no post in London on Sunday, I was kept waiting till Monday. I " would be making myself uneasy again!"—and at the time I read that letter, she was already dead! On the Mon-

day came no letter from her as promised, but
one from the Dr., stating her to be dangerously
ill, yet not precluding all hope, for he feared the
blow for me, altho' at the time he wrote he had
no hope himself. Of course I set out by the next
railway train, not despairing—oh no, or I *could*
not have gone. I thought I had little hope; but
when all hope was taken from me, I found that I
had had much. You know the rest. I travelled
all night in the cruellest suspense, and arriving
in Liverpool in the morning, was told that my
Uncle and Walter were already gone to her
funeral! Oh, Bess, is it not a wonder that I
kept my senses? I am better in health now, but
still very feeble and nervous, and so sad! Oh,
there is such a perpetual weight on my heart as
I cannot describe to you. I feel as helpless and
desolate as a little child turned adrift in the
world! I who have so many friends! But what
are friends? What is a husband even, compared
with one's Mother? Of *her* love one is always so
sure! It is the only love that nothing—not even
misconduct on our part—can take away from us.

If the letter I began went to you, I have said all this before, for it is the only sort of thing I have to say to any one, and accordingly I write none at all except to the few whose sympathy I have perfect confidence in.

When shall I see you again? here, I mean; for I do not think I shall ever have the heart to set foot in Scotland any more. Alas! alas! what a changed Scotland for me—a place of graves!

My sweet little Cousin Jeannie[1] is still here with me—a comfort so far [as] any companionship *can be* a comfort to me.

Write to me, dear Eliza, and do not mind my silences. That I thought of you much during *this time* is a sufficient proof of the constancy of [my?] regard.

Ever your affectionate
JANE CARLYLE.

---

[1] Her cousin from Liverpool (*Letters and Memorials*, i., p. 145).

LIV.

Extract from Letter to Mrs. Pringle.

5 CHEYNE ROW, CHELSEA.

[Late in 1858.]

MY DEAR MRS. PRINGLE,—

* * * * *

It is rather vexatious, don't you think? to have gone and laid myself up so early in the winter. It was Lord Ashburton's *Picture* that was the innocent ostensible cause. I told you, I think, of the beautiful Picture of little Fritz and his sister Wilhelmina,[1] which Lord A. *would* give me, and which I had no place for in all

---

[1] A plate entitled, "The Little Drummer," and described as being "engraved by Francis Hall from a copy in Lord Ashburton's possession of the picture at Charlottenburg by Antoine Pesne," forms the frontispiece to vol. i. of Carlyle's *Frederick the Great*, of which the first two volumes appeared in September of this year; and in Book vi., chap. vi., will be found Carlyle's description of the picture. He bequeathed this "large oil painting" to Lord Ashburton's widow and daughter. (See the codicil to his will in Norton's edition of the *Reminiscences*, i., p. 276.)

my house, unless I removed the great bookcase from the drawing-room to the room below. It was sent on his return to London, exactly at the wrong moment, when the weather had become intensely cold : at least at the wrong moment, when there was a remarkably impatient Husband in the case. *I* would have let it stand on the parlour floor, for my part, until there was fitter weather for a household earthquake. But every day Mr. C. suggested, "My Dear, when are you thinking of," etc. ? "Is the paper made yet for that wall ?" "Are you *never* going to," etc., etc. ? till mortal patience could stand it no longer ! and I sent for the carpenter and the paperhanger, and the staircase window had to be taken out, and all the doors flying, and myself flying to direct blockheads, for a whole day. So at night I went to bed in a high fever—quite another sort of "fever" from any *you* ever saw me in—and for three successive nights I never closed my eyes, and was in agonies of face-ache, etc., etc., and now I am shut up for six months, I expect, with my *cough*, and all the rest of it.

But the cough is not so bad as last year, and I have more *strength* to bear it—thanks to Bay House and Lann Hall.[2] Pity there is no sunshine in this world without shadow. That Picture is very charming to look at from my sofa, but *such* a cold is a heavy price for the pleasure! I remember, as if it were yesterday, travelling all night in a postchaise with my Mother and an old East Lothian farmer, who was going to meet my Father at Craigenputtoch, and advise about *drains*. My Mother and I were to be dropt at my Grandfather's. I was mad with joy to go on my *first* journey, but oh, so *sick* in a close carriage always! one minute I was chattering like a magpie, the next, vomiting out of the window. In the course of the night I lay down at the bottom of the chaise, my head on my Mother's knees, and whimpered and moaned. The old farmer got tired of me—naturally—and said, with a certain sharpness, words that cut into my small heart with a sudden, mysterious

---

[2] Cf. *Letters and Memorials*, ii., pp. 365, 377.

horror. "Little girl," he said, "don't you know there is no pleasure to be had in this world without pain?" No, I didn't know it. But it was dreadful to hear; for, somehow, I thought he who was *old* must be speaking truth, and I believed him, all in shrinking from him as a sort of cruel ogre!

That was *my* initiation into the dark side of life. What was yours?

Now good-night.

Love to the boys. Is the nursemaid gone to fulfil her Destiny?

Affectionately yours,

JANE C. WELSH[3]—

Oh, I mean Jane W. Carlyle!

---

[3] Cf. signature to Letter XXXIV., p. 215.

LV.

[*No address preserved.—To the Rev. D. Aitken, 4 Charlotte Square, Edinburgh.*]

5 CHEYNE ROW, CHELSEA,
15*th March* [1866].

THANKS, dear Mr. Aitken, your kind letter[1] made our *Breakfast* this morning quite pleasant! and in cases of bad sleepers, it takes a good deal to do *that*, as you may perhaps know!

It was indeed a most agreeable surprise, to receive such a friendly letter from you and Eliza! The more shame to—which of us that it should have *surprised* as well as pleased?

But there is no time to go into *that*, at the present writing!

---

[1] This is the letter referred to in *Letters and Memorials of Jane Welsh Carlyle*, iii., p. 313. "One of the letters of invitation I had quite surprised me by its warmth and eagerness, being from a quarter where I hardly believed myself remembered—David Aitken and Eliza Stodart! They had both grown into sticks, I was thinking." Dr. Aitken had resigned the living of Minto in 1864, and gone to live in Edinburgh.

That we cannot either or both of us accept your friendly invitation so cordially given, makes no difference in our gratification at receiving it.

Mr. C. has already engaged himself, it seems to me, to *five* different places!! and lastly and most particularly to our old Friend Thomas Erskine. What reason he (Mr. C.) has for believing that he will be safer from railway whistles (!) in Mr. Erskine's house than in any other in Edinburgh or about it, I really don't know; but *that* does seem to be the consideration which is directing his choice![2]

As for me, I have taken fright at the cold weather, the long journey, and the fuss and agitation of attending my Husband thro' an operation little more agreeable to him than being

---

[2] In the letter (to one of her aunts) quoted in the previous note, she also says: "Mr. C. is going to stay, while in Edinburgh, at Thomas Erskine's, our dear old friend; not, however, because of liking him better than any one else there, but because of his being most out of the way of— railway whistles!" Mr. Erskine, of Linlathen, was then living at 11 Great Stuart Street, from which he dates a letter on March 30th, asking Dr. and Mrs. Aitken for the following Monday "to meet your friend Mr. Carlyle."

hanged! Indeed, I am sure many a thick-skinned Palmer or Pritchard[3] have had the rope "adjusted" about their necks with less horror than poor Mr. C. will let them put that "robe and cap" on him![4]

"What the eye sees not the heart grieves not!"

So I mean to keep at a safe distance.

My kind love to Eliza, whom I hope to see some day, tho' not just now. How I should like a long, long talk with her about "dear old long ago"! What would she think of *asking me* in the warm weather? I am not bad at travelling now, in ordinary circumstances! indeed, I have been better *last* winter than for *many* preceding ones, tho' I *couldn't* go to Miss R——'s evening parties!

Yours affl͞y, with thanks
And kind regards from Mr. C.,
JANE W. CARLYLE.

---

[3] Physicians and poisoners, of Rugeley and Glasgow, hanged in 1856 and 1865 respectively.

[4] At his installation as Lord Rector of Edinburgh University.

THE RUINED CHANCEL OF HADDINGTON CHURCH, WITH THE GRAVE ✝ OF DR. WELSH AND MRS. CARLYLE.

From a Photograph by W. H. Wildridge, of Haddington.

[*Face p. 1.*]

[Mrs. Carlyle died on Saturday, April 21st, 1866, and was buried, according to her early wish (see Letter I.) and "according to covenant of forty years back,"[5] in the same grave with her father.]

---

[5] Carlyle, *Reminiscences*, ed. Norton, i., p. 254; Froude, *Thomas Carlyle*, B. ii., p. 316. It is strange that Carlyle says "in the nave of the old Abbey Kirk." The grave is in the chancel.

ADDENDA TO THE NOTES.

Page 12, *note* 5. For an account of John Barclay and his Museum, see Prof. Struthers' *Historical Sketch of the Edinburgh Anatomical School* (Edin., 1867), pp. 56-70. The Museum contained skeletons of the elephant, boar, camel, etc. Jane Welsh may have been taken by her father to see these curiosities.

Page 35, *note* 10. An account of George Rennie will be found in *Men of the Reign* (edited by T. H. Ward, London, 1885), from which Carlyle's remarks may be supplemented. He "was in early life a sculptor, and produced in Rome some remarkable works, of which the 'Grecian Archer' he presented to the Athenæum Club. In 1836 he suggested to Mr. William Ewart, M.P., the Parliamentary Committee which led to the formation of schools of design, and in conjunction with Mr. Joseph Hume, M.P., he secured free access for students to the public art galleries in London. In 1841 Mr. Rennie was returned for Ipswich in the Liberal interest; but retired at the ensuing general election in favour of the local candidate. Shortly afterwards he was offered the government of the Falkland Islands, a colony he succeeded in raising from the most abject condition to one of the greatest prosperity. He died in London, March 22nd, 1860."

Page 39, line 8. "Joseph," named along with Chantry, is probably Samuel Joseph, R.S.A., a sculptor who died in 1850. See *Men of the Reign*.

Page 84, *note* 5. A portrait of "The Tiger" appeared in *Fraser* and will be found in *The Maclise Portrait Gallery*, ed. by William Bates (1883), p. 163. It is a most admirable drawing, and brings out a likeness between his head and the picture of a Tiger's head on the wall. From the very brief account of William Dunlop, it appears that he was an Edinburgh medical man who went to London in 1825. In 1826 he assisted John Galt in the formation of the Canada Company, and went out with him to Ontario. In 1832 he published *Letters of a Backwoodsman*. Probably the "Wull" referred to as a man "with brains in his head" in Letter V. (p. 25) is the same person.

Page 90, 91. I suppose this cousin James Baillie must be the "Captain Baillie," Miss Jewsbury's account of whom has been omitted by Mr. Froude and also by Prof. Norton, who mentions the omission in his edition of the *Reminiscences*, i., p. 62, *note*.

INDEX OF PROPER NAMES.

Roman numerals denote Letters; Arabic numerals denote pages; *n* means that the reference is only to the Editor's notes. For incidents and details, see the Table of Contents.

AITKEN, Rev. David, Letters of Carlyle to, XVIII., XIX., XXV., XXVI., XLVII., XLVIII., XLIX.; Letter of Mrs. Carlyle to, LV.; Letter of Carlyle about, XXXI.; *Pref.* p. viii., 270.
Aitken, James, 32, 307.
Aitken, Sam., Letter to, from Carlyle, XXXI.; *Pref.* p. viii.; 8, 12, 58 *n.*, 166, 170, 288 *n.*
Ainsley, W., 45.
Alfieri, 70.
Annan, Visit to, 311 *n.*
Ashburton, Lord, 322.
Austin, Mrs., 267, 270.
BAILLIE, James, 90-92, 97 *n.*, 103, 104, 114, 330 *n.*
"Baillie" in name of Jane Welsh, 92, 93 *n.*, 96.
Baillie's Letters, 292, 297.
Bannatyne Club, 298.
Barclay Museum, 12.
Barjarg Library, 250.
Blackwood's Magazine, 49.
Boreland, 62.
Bradfute, John, Letters of Carlyle to, *P.S.* to XXX. (191), XLIII.; *Pref.* p. vii., 203 *n.*, 288.
Brewster, Sir David, 159.
British Museum, 292.
Bullers (Carlyle's pupils), 58, 60 *n.*
Byron, Lord, 30, 101; Verses on, by Jane Welsh, 102 *n.*
CAMBRIDGE University Library, 292, 298.
Campan's *Memoirs of Marie Antoinette*, 251.
Carlisle, 15, 18.
Carlton Street, Edinburgh, 219 *n.*; XXXVIII. (232).
Carlyle, Alexander, 137.
Carlyle, Dr. John, 88, 138, 158, 244, 310 (?).
Carlyle, Margaret, 141.
Carlyle, Thomas, Letters of, XVIII., XIX., XXV., XXVI., *P.S.* to XXX., XXXI., XXXVI., XXXVII., XLIII., XLVII., XLVIII., XLIX. More important references to, in Letters of Jane Welsh Carlyle, 34, 42, 58, 60 *n.*, 77 (?), 78, 85, 89 (?), 100, 101, 107-109,114,117, 118,137, 139, 140, 144, 150, 152, 201, 202, 230, 234, 248, 249, 250, 252, 280, 283, 284, 301, 302, 306, 323, 327, 328; Carlyle's father, 213 *n.*; Carlyle's grandmother, 187; his *Frederick the Great*, 291 *n.*, 322 *n.*; *French Revolution*, 258, 280, 283, 284, 313 *n*; *German Literature*, projected *History of*, XXV., XXVI.; Lectures on, 283, 284; *On Heroes*, 298 *n.*; *Sartor Resartus*, 312 *n.* Mr. Scot Skirving's interview with, 315 *n.*, 316 *n.*
Chalmers, Rev. Dr., 37, 59.
Chantry, 39.
Charteris, Hon. Francis, 315.
Chelsea (5 Cheyne Row). House described by Carlyle, 256, 257; by Mrs. Carlyle, 266; Letters written from, XLIII. to end.
Chelsea Hospital, 267.
Cicero, 74.
Clare, Countess of, 244.
Cochrane (Editor of *Foreign Quarterly*), 185.
Coleridge, Death of, 258, 259.
Comely Bank, Edinburgh; Letters from, XVIII., XIX.; 202, 263.
Cooke, the actor, 251.
Cooper's Novels, 231.
Craigenputtoch, Letters written from, XX.-XXXIV., XXXVII., XXXIX.-XLII.; more important references to, 23 *n.*, 129, 132, 136, 158,166, 171,174, 191, 237, 265, 324.
Crichtons, of Dabton, 65.
Cunningham, George, 45.
DARWIN, Erasmus, 309.
Degli Antoni, Countess, 279.
De Staël, Madame, 76, 251.
Disraeli, Benjamin, 316 *n.*
Dodds (? Dods), Peter, 51.
Donaldson, Alexander, 152; The Donaldsons, 245, 303 *n.*
Dumfries, 63, 131, 170, 204.
Dundas, Henry (Viscount Melville), 194.
Dunlop, William (the "Tiger"), 84 *n.*, 171 *n.*, 330 *n.*
EDINBURGH, 130, 149, 260, 285, 327, 328; University Library, 165.
Erskine, Thomas, of Linlathen, 327.
FLEMING, Dr., 58.
Fraser's Magazine, 286.
Frederick the Great, Carlyle's, 291 *n.*, 322 *n.*
French Revolution, Carlyle's, 258, 280, 283, 284, 313 *n.*
Fyffe, Dr., 25, 78, 87, 108, 189, 190.

INDEX OF PROPER NAMES.

GALL (the phrenologist), 56.
Geddes, Jenny, 295.
George IV., visit to Edinburgh, 67 n., 73 n.
German Literature, Carlyle's projected *History of*, XXV., XXVI.; Lectures on, 283, 284.
Gillies, R. Pearse, 85.
Goethe, 63, 100, 101, 124-126, 132.
"Good Intent, The" (coach), 67.
Graham, William, 137.
HADDINGTON, Letters from, I.-III., V.-VIII., X.-XII., XIV., XV.; more important references to, 19-21, 189, 277, 307, 309; the church of, 5, 303 n., 316 n.
Hamilton, Count Anthony, 162 n.
Hamilton, Sir William, 159.
Howden, Thomas, 86, 89.
Hunt, Leigh, 267, 270.
Hunter-Arundell, Mr., of Barjarg, 250 n.
Hunter, Rev. John, 250.
Hunter, Susan, 278.
INGLIS, Henry, 138, 202, 244.
Irving, Edward, 29 n., 58, 65, 110, 177 n., 223.
JEFFREY, Francis, 133, 137, 138, 140, 149, 178, 194, 195, 197, 231, 254.
Jewsbury, Miss, 57 n., 315 n.
Joseph, Samuel (sculptor), 39, 330 n.
Julius, Dr., 124.
KEITH, Sir Alexander (Knight-Marischal), 81, 82.
Kemble, Fanny, 287.
Kiallmark, 104.
LARDNER, Dr., 155 n.
Lee, Principal, 295.
Libraries, 292, 293.
Liverpool, Letter from, IV.; 17, 253, 320.
London, 195, 199, 284, 285, 299, 301.
Lorimer, Rev. R., 3.
MACTURK, R., 15, 32.
Martineau, Harriet, 231, 232, 286, 287.
Mazzini, Joseph, 305 n., 306.
Mill, J. S., 270.
Minto, Lord, 122 n., 243.
Moffat, visit to, 247.
Moir, George (Professor), 150, 151.
Montagu, Mrs. Basil, 262.
Montrose (M. Napier's *Life of*), 295.
Moore's *Irish Melodies*, 74.
Moray Street, Edinburgh, 85.
Murray, Dr. Thomas, 297.
NAPIER, Mark, 295.
PENFILLAN, 62, 111 n.
Popoli, Count, 278, 279.
Peterkin, A., 290, 294.
Pringle, Mrs., Letter to, LIV.

Procter, B. W. (Barry Cornwall), 101.
RABELAIS, phrase wrongly ascribed to, by Carlyle, 162.
Rennie, George, 32, 35, 38-42, 54, 55, 82, 88, 268-270, 277, 300, 307, 329 n.
Richardson, Mrs., 138.
Richmond (?), Duke of, 174.
Ritchie, Rev. D., 57: his account of Jane Welsh's "Tragedy," 57 n.
Roland, Madame, 251.
Rousseau's *La Nouvelle Héloïse*, 29-35, 37, 38.
Ruffini, Augustine, 309.
Ruffini, Giovanni, 305.
Russell, Lord John, 194.
Russell, Dr., 207, 319.
SANDWICH Islands, King and Queen of, 240.
Sapio (opera singer), 227.
Sartor Resartus, allusion to, 312.
Schiller, 68, 70, 76.
Scot, Miss, Letter to, LI.
Seton, Mrs., 9.
Shandy (Miss Welsh's dog), 60.
Skirving, Mr. Scot, Letter to, LII.; Reminiscences of Carlyle and Mrs. Carlyle, 303 n., 311 n., 315 n.
Somerville, Mary, 267.
Sophocles, *Philoctetes* of, 316 n.
Spalding, John, 295.
Spurzheim, 56.
Sterling, John, 278.
Sterne's "starling," 19, 291.
Stevenson, Andrew, 293 (and *note*), 298.
Strathmilligau, 15, 16.
TAIT, George (bookseller in Haddington), 49, 54 n.
Templand, Letters from, IX., XIII., XVI., XVII., XXXV., XXXVI.
Terrot, Rev. C. H. (Bishop of Edinburgh), 271.
Turner, Sir James, 298.
VEITCH, Captain, 308.
WAUGH (publisher), 49, 294.
Welsh, Dr. John (Jane Welsh's father), 2, 4-6, 9, 10, 16, 237, 238, 303 n., 324, 329 n.
Welsh, John (maternal uncle), 17, 61.
Welsh, Mrs. (her mother), more important references to, 1, 25, 27, 47, 61, 85, 130, 139, 179, 190, 197, 207, 213, 214, 238, 244, 271, 279, 317-320, 324.
Welsh, Robert (paternal uncle), 3, 11, 16, 67, 71, 137, 275.
Welsh, Walter (maternal grandfather), 210 n.
Wemyss, Earl of, 315 n.
Whittaker (publisher), 155 n.

www.ingramcontent.com/pod-product-compliance
Lightning Source LLC
Chambersburg PA
CBHW020220240426
43672CB00006B/364